ISBN: 0-9543374-4-1

The Association of Photographers
81 Leonard Street, London EC2A 4QS
Tel: +44 (0)20 7739 6669
Fax: +44 (0)20 7739 8707
E-mail: general@aophoto.co.uk
Website: www.the-aop.org

Managing Director   Rod Varley
Awards Manager   Nicola Waterhouse
Design & Production   Jonathan Briggs
Printing & Colour Management   Magnet Harlequin

CONTENTS

[magnet harlequin]

Magnet Harlequin is truly delighted to be sponsoring the Photography Awards 2004 Book. The stunning photography you are about to see showcases the creative talents of the finest practitioners of the photographer's art, and therefore needs no further endorsement from us. But the end result is only half the story as the journey from camera to printed page requires immense know-how and skill if the final printed image is to achieve the standards you see here.

We've been in the colour business for 23 years, reproducing images to meet the standards of the most discerning of critics – photographers themselves. Along the way we've acquired a seasoned eye and it is a credit to all whose work is shown here that we can still be taken aback by their creative art. We have always understood both the photographer's intent and the printer's craft, and, as such, it has been a privilege to apply our own standards of high-end Colour Management, Pre-Press and Print Production to this project.

In summary, to all those whose photography is featured in these awards, many congratulations. To be successful in this hugely respected event is something to be particularly proud of. It has been our pleasure to reproduce your work.

Enjoy.

www.magharl.co.uk

PHOTOGRAPHY AWARDS 2004

The Photography Awards are organised by the AOP, a not-for-profit organisation originally formed in London in 1968 as the Association of Fashion & Advertising Photographers. Today, it brings together professional photographers to protect their rights and promote photography and, as image-makers respond to globalisation, it has members worldwide building an effective network of communications with photographers for the 21st Century.

The images in this book represent some of greatest photographs produced over the last 18 months and include the prestigious AOP Photographers' Awards for AOP members, the Fujifilm Assistants' Awards and the Zeitgeist – a revealing new section in which leading industry figures select the images which, for them, sum-up where commercial photography is today.

Whilst the AOP is primarily an organisation for commercial photographers working in the advertising, design, fashion and editorial arenas, our members' work goes far beyond that which appears in public. Professional photographers represent one of the great unsung sources of exceptional creative talent, and contained within these pages is also the personal work of those artists. This is exceptionally pertinent to the creative industries and visual culture today, where the traditional boundaries between commercial and fine art is becoming increasingly less distinct.

So whilst primarily a celebration and recognition of great photographers and their images, it is also a snapshot of our photographic times, judged, curated and compiled by people who are earning their living and care about photography.

Resolution Creative

It's a great feeling being creative. The joy of building something that comes from the heart and giving it to the world for people to enjoy. It's not always about production for the sake of sale, but often rather about love, and about art.

Resolution Creative is about blending your love of creativity with our love of creative production.

We are a team of creative printers, designers, photographers and digital experts offering something more than a conventional 'lab' service. In a town that can often leave you feeling remote from the production process, we want you to know that we don't just press buttons and send you a bill at the end. We like to see ourselves as not just part of the process, but rather partners in the process.

Resolution Creative is West London's newest home of creative production and, in conjunction with Epson, are proud to be associated with the AOP as major sponsors of the 2004 Awards.

It's time to enjoy being creative again.

Bruce Mitchell

www.resolveandcreate.co.uk

EPSON®

The photographic community continually aspires to capture exceptional images and then reproduce them in many innovative and beautiful ways. At EPSON we aim to produce the highest quality photographic output for professional photographers. We do this through the development of our professional photo-inkjet printer range, Ultrachrome inks and range of specialist medias including photo and fine art papers.

We are extremely proud to have been chosen as the preferred photo printer manufacturer to produce the exhibition prints for the Photography Awards 2004. This accolade reinforces the success of our products within the photographic market.

Congratulations to all photographers whose work has been included in this book. It is through sharing these innovative and exceptional images with others that makes the subject of photography so rewarding.

Raj Parmar
Marketing Manager

21ST AOP

PHOTOGRAPHERS'

AWARDS

THE JUDGES

Left to right from back:

Nigel Clifton, Sophie Batterbury,
Nadav Kander, Tim Flach, Suzanne Bisset,
Desmond Burdon, Simon Norfolk, Alan Dye

Nigel Clifton >

Nigel Clifton is a creative director at EHS Brann, an agency which integrates on and off line thinking for clients as diverse as British Gas, Tesco, Habitat, Diesel and egg. He studied at London College of Printing and Birmingham Institute of Art and Design, a journey encompassing typography, graphic, furniture and interior design. Although a regular commissioner of original photography, his own pursuit of the craft is limited to weekend dabbling.

Sophie Batterbury >

Sophie Batterbury has worked primarily for Independent Newspapers since 1989, when she joined the darkroom as a b/w printer. As production methods changed and the paper moved to colour photography she moved to working with Photoshop and became Night Picture Editor. After a brief tenure at WENN in 1998 she returned to *The Independent* to become picture editor of the Daily Review features section. In 2001 she become Associate Picture Editor (Sunday) with sole responsibility for pictures in *The Independent on Sunday* newspaper sections. In her spare(!) time she is also a contributing picture editor of *Ei8ht Magazine*.

< Suzanne Bisset

Scottish born Suzanne Bisset opened her first gallery in Dublin, at the age of 19. After working with the likes of U2 and the KLF she moved into films in Wales before stopping off for a few years in Bristol to work in arts journalism, and then eventually moving to London to Dazed & Confused. However, her love for photography saw her curate the 'My Cup of Tea' project, the critically acclaimed book and touring exhibition in aid of Cancer Research UK. Suzanne, now Director of her own arts agency Art Official, is currently touring the photography exhibition 'The Rolling Stones & The Beatles' to UK Museums & Paris & Milan.

< Desmond Burdon

Desmond has been a professional photographer for over 30 years. During this time, he has worked on just about every product from engagement rings to Jumbo Jets. Desmond was involved in setting up the awards 20 years ago, was the chairman for six years, on the awards committee for a further four years, and is the only photographer who has ever personally sponsored the event. He has now decided to stop working in commercial photography and is moving to New Zealand to concentrate on his personal photographs and his young family. He was so delighted and honored to be asked to judge the awards as a final salute to the AOP.

21ST AOP
PHOTOGRAPHERS'
AWARDS

< Nadav Kander

Nadav Kander was born in Israel in 1961. He grew up in South Africa from 1964 and then moved to London in the mid 80s. Nadav now resides in London with his wife and three children.

Kander is one of the most highly respected photographers in his field, recently undertaking commissions for Air France, Adidas, Heals, Levis, Nike, Piper Heidsieck & The Big Issue (amongst others). He also regularly contributes to Dazed & Confused, Blackbook, Exit, Tank, Q, Viewpoint & the Observer Magazine. Nadav exhibits and sells his work through galleries worldwide and his work forms part of the public collection at the National Portrait Gallery and V&A, London.

< Tim Flach

Tim Flach is a photographer working mainly in advertising and stock, as well as personal projects. He specialises in wild animals mostly taken in the studio, with a particular interest in their anthropomorphic qualities. He is represented by agents in New York, London and Paris. Tim is presently Chair of the Awards committee.

Simon Norfolk >

After leaving the Documentary Photography course in Newport, South Wales, Simon worked for left-wing publications specialising in work on anti-racist activities and fascist groups. In 1994 he gave up photojournalism in favour of landscape photography and his book, *For Most Of It I Have No Words*, about the landscapes of the places that have seen genocide, was published in 1998 to wide approval. In 2001, he also began a major project on the relationship between war and landscape, taking him to the wars in Afghanistan and Iraq; to Israel and Palestine; and to refugee camps in Ingushetia, Chad, Lebanon and Pakistan. The work from Afghanistan won the European Publishers' Award for Photography in 2002.

Alan Dye >

Alan Dye graduated from Maidstone College of Art in 1990 with a BA Hons in Graphic Design. He worked for a number of agencies including Roundel Design Group, Lambie Nairn and Pentagram Design. It was at Pentagram that Alan met his two partners, Nick Finney and Ben Stott, and founded NB:Studio in 1997. Recent clients include The Royal Mail, Boots the Chemist, Tate Modern, The National Portrait Gallery, Universal Pictures, Investors Chronicle and The Royal Academy of Arts.

21ST AOP PHOTOGRAPHERS' AWARDS

We have great pleasure in sponsoring the Portraits category of the 21st Awards. As ever, we are dedicated to supporting the art of the photographer, and whole-heartedly endorse the enthusiasm, commitment and technical excellence demonstrated at these awards.

Ben Richardson
Managing Director – Metro Imaging Ltd

PORTRAITS

SINGLE

SIMON BURCH   **SILVER**

PRINTER: Conor Timmons at   TITLE: Mask
Primary Colour, Dublin   CASTING: Patrick Daly

ROBERT WILSON   **MERIT**
PRINTER: Robert Wilson   TITLE: Bill

VICTOR ALBROW

PRINTER: Hamish at Altered Images   TITLE: Lachie and Callum

MATT BARLOW

Title: Jim

ANDY BARTER

PRINTER: Andy Barter   TITLE: Chin Up

SIMON BURCH

PRINTER: Conor Timmons at
Primary Colour, Dublin

TITLE: Vincent
CASTING: Patrick Daly

RORY CARNEGIE

PRINTER: Augustine Norbert
at Flash Photo Digital
TITLE: Zombie

CLIENT: Infogrammes
ART DIRECTOR: Rob Perham
at Mercier Gray
STYLIST: Karen Smith

CHRIS FRAZER-SMITH

PRINTER: Chris Frazer-Smith   TITLE: Jaques, Paris

NICK IVINS

PRINTER: Pip at Gone Wild
CLIENT: The Erotic Review

COMMISSIONED BY:
Rowan Pelling & Gavin Griffiths
ART DIRECTOR:
Bella Pringle at Gone Wild

ANDREW MONTGOMERY

PRINTER: Roy Snell Fine Art Digital   TITLE: Gypsy Woman
CLIENT: Country Living

ROBERT WILSON

PRINTER: Robert Wilson   TITLE: Phyllis

MEL YATES

PRINTER: Kevin McDonagh at Keishi   ART DIRECTOR: Nathalie Goldstein
TITLE: Martin & Fred   CLIENT: Getty Images

PORTRAITS

SERIES

MARC GOUBY   SILVER

PRINTER: Jean-Pierre Haie,   COMMISSIONED BY: TBWA Paris
Atelier Demi Teinte   ART DIRECTOR: Jorge Careño
TITLE: Veterans   SYSTEM OPERATOR: Fred Perrot
CLIENT: Playstation, Sony   at La Retoucherie

ANDREAS SMETANA　　　　　　　　　　　　**MERIT**

PRINTER: Andreas Smetana　　　COMMISSIONED BY:
TITLE: Heineken Long Neck　　　Leo Burnett Sydney
CLIENT: Heineken　　　　　　　ART DIRECTOR: Jason Williams

gettyimages®

Getty Images is proud to sponsor The Awards as they turn 21, and congratulates the Association of Photographers in having achieved a rare balance – an event that is both established and yet remains vital. The imagery that we all strive to create, whether in commercial or personal spheres, has the emotional immediacy to educate, entertain, inspire and challenge us – it is our visual language. We salute the photographers who –collected in this book – have helped expand our shared vocabulary.

Lewis Blackwell
Senior Vice President – Creative Direction

LIFE

SINGLE

NICK GEORGHIOU   MERIT

PRINTER: Bayeux   COMMISSIONED BY: RKCR/Y and R
TITLE: Landrover Maasai   ART DIRECTOR: Jerry Hollens
CLIENT: Landrover   SYSTEM OPERATOR: Spence at Actis

PAUL MURPHY   MERIT

PRINTER: Paul Murphy
TITLE: Hold Up
CLIENT: Volkswagon
COMMISSIONED BY: BMPDDB

ART DIRECTOR:
Fergal Ballance & Nick Allsop
SYSTEM OPERATOR: James Digby-Jones
at Saddington Baynes

MEL YATES   MERIT

PRINTER: Kevin McDonagh at Keishi   TITLE: Mia & Marianne
                                         CLIENT: Getty Images

LOTTIE DAVIES

PRINTER: Suki at Salamander   TITLE: Parshall, Colorado

MARK DAVISON

TITLE: Bowling Alley, Prague

DOUG MENUEZ

TITLE: The Half King

PAOLO PATRIZI

PRINTER: Paolo Patrizi   TITLE: Houshi Onsen, Japan

KULBIR THANDI

PRINTER: Kulbir Thandi   TITLE: Beach
                                SYSTEM OPERATOR: Lee Rouse

LIFE

SERIES

KIRAN MASTER   **SILVER**

PRINTER: Ian at The Print Room

ERWIN OLAF   SILVER

TITLE: Separation 1 – Separation 3 –   SYSTEM OPERATOR:
Separation 4 – Separation 5   Wieger Poutsma at Fisk Imaging

21st AOP Photographers' Awards

DAVID STEWART   MERIT

PRINTER: David Stewart
TITLE: Farmers, Thong, Bull
(Malvern Water)
COMMISSIONED BY: Lowe

ART DIRECTOR:
Christian Cotterill/Justin Hooper
SYSTEM OPERATOR: John Swift,
The Colour Company

MARK DAVISON

PRINTER: Mark Davison
TITLE: Shoeshine – Texas,

Barbershop – Texas,
Quick Lunch Diner – Texas

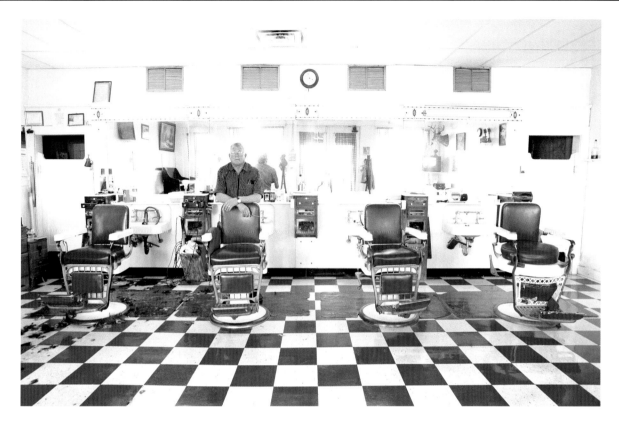

CLARE PARK

PRINTER: Robin Bell   TITLE: Ysabelle's Mask 2003

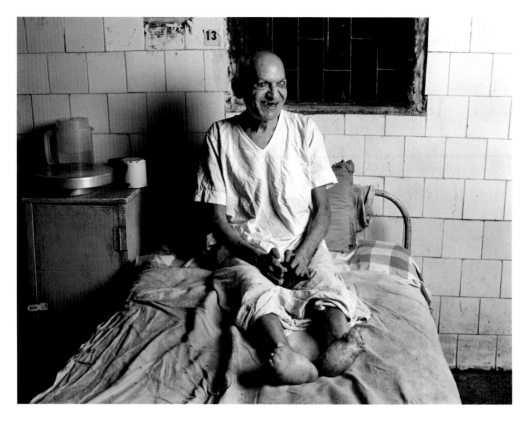

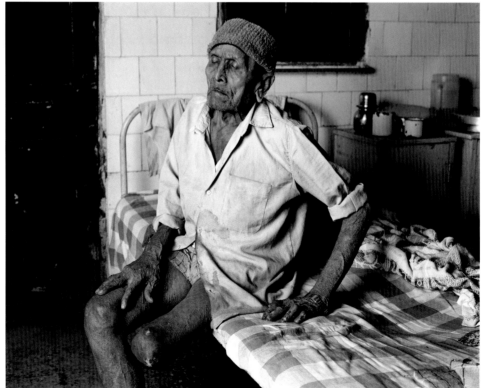

KERENA PERRONET-MILLER

PRINTER: Graeme Bulcraig
at Touch Digital

TITLE: Leprosy

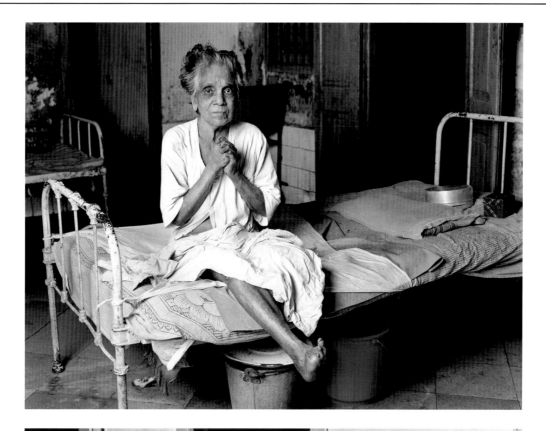

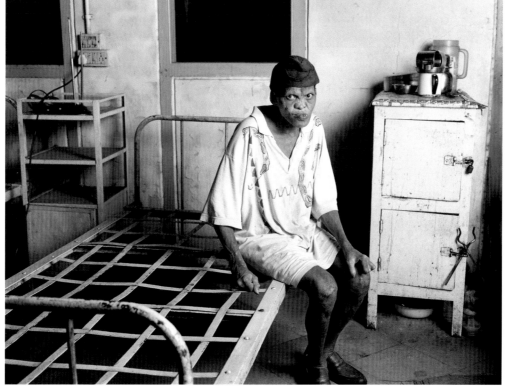

SIMON STOCK

PRINTER: Simon Stock
TITLE: Yukon Eskimo

CLIENT: Shell North America
COMMISSIONED BY: JWT Houston
ART DIRECTOR: Bob Braun

JAAP VLIEGENTHART

PRINTER:
René Bierman at Souverein

SYSTEM OPERATOR:
Rutger Luijs at Souvereign
TITLE: Occult Encounters

z e f a

Zefa visual media, the largest picture library network in Europe, is proud to support the Association of Photographers Awards for the second year running. zefa provides creative, fresh, contemporary stock photography that meets only the highest professional standards.

Following the developments and trends in photography is an astonishing and fascinating experience. We are passionate about the future of photography and congratulate the winners of this award. We hope that they continue in their drive to inspire us with fresh and innovative perspectives.

Siri Vorbeck
Creative Director – zefa visual media

SOCIETY

SINGLE

ANDREAS SMETANA   SILVER
PRINTER: Andreas Smetana   TITLE: Soldiers At The Forbidden City

JULIA FULLERTON-BATTEN   **MERIT**

TITLE: Gran Canaria

RAINER STRATMANN   MERIT

PRINTER: Rainer Stratmann   SYSTEM OPERATOR:
CLIENT: KNAUFinsulation   Studio Wolfgang Scheit

JENS HONORE

TITLE: Stalingrad   SYSTEM OPERATOR: Werkstette

JENS HONORE

TITLE: Chernobyl
CLIENT: Ojo de pez

COMMISSIONED BY: Arianna Rinaldo
SYSTEM OPERATOR: Werkstette

ANTHONY MARSLAND

PRINTER: Anthony Marsland   CLIENT: Getty
TITLE: Where's it gone?   ART DIRECTOR: Paul Foster

JAAP VLIEGENTHART

PRINTER: René Bierman at Souverein   SYSTEM OPERATOR:
TITLE: Unchained   Hans Berg Huis at Souverein

21st AOP PHOTOGRAPHERS' AWARDS

SOCIETY

SERIES

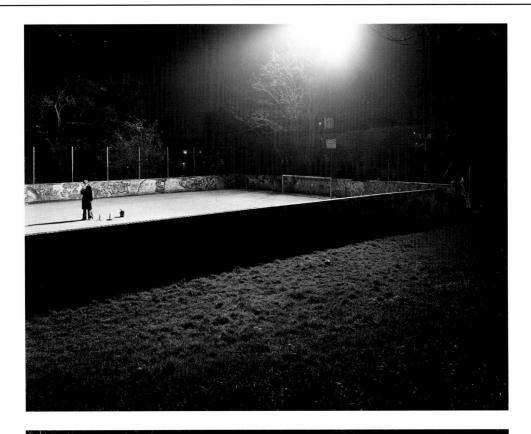

DYLAN COLLARD

PRINTER: Goldenshot Digital
STYLIST: Mim Quin-Harkin
OTHER: Thanks to Helen & Neil,
Christian, Sam & Tim, Ju, Andres &
Chris, Karen, Charlie boy & Charlie girl,

Ali, Ben, Pete, Phil, Piet, Allan, Matt,
Adam, for assistance and modelling,
all at Goldenshot and Taylor James for
help and encouragement

ADAM HINTON

TITLE: The Favela, Rio De Janeiro, Brazil

photographers and advertisers in the UK and many names in Europe and the USA.
Whatever else has changed, our founding premise remains the same –
our objective is always to make your assignment a success.

FASHION

SINGLE

MORRISON/VAN VALEN   MERIT

PRINTER: Adrian Van Valen   TITLE: Breeze
                                   SYSTEM OPERATOR: Adrian Van Valen

DAVID SHORT   **MERIT**

TITLE: Harriet   HAIR & MAKE-UP: Leanne Shaw

TIM MacPHERSON

PRINTER: Tim MacPherson   ART DIRECTOR: Sarah Cromwell

21st AOP

PHOTOGRAPHERS'
AWARDS

SPONSORED BY

MOT MODELS

FASHION

+

SERIES

PEER LINDGREEN

PRINTER: Peer Lindgreen   TITLE: Ivana Mlačić

ALAN MAHON

PRINTER: Alan Mahon

ART DIRECTOR & STYLIST:
Steven Claydon

LANDSCAPE

SINGLE

DAVID HARRIMAN   MERIT

PRINTER: Jo Stout   SYSTEM OPERATOR: Nadege Meriau

CHRISTIAN SCHMIDT   **MERIT**

PRINTER: Etizy Baris

BOB ELSDALE

PRINTER: Bob Elsdale
TITLE: Hornbeam in Snow

CLIENT: Getty Images
COMMISSIONED BY: Getty Images
ART DIRECTOR: Sabine Davis

SIMON HARSENT

PRINTER: Simon Harsent   TITLE: Forest

VËRONIQUE ROLLAND

PRINTER:
John Cleur at The Printroom

TITLE: Buenos Aires

21st AOP Photographers' Awards

ANDY SMITH

PRINTER: Andy Smith

TITLE: Car Park
SYSTEM OPERATOR: Jonathan Kitchen

SIMON STOCK

PRINTER: Simon Stock   TITLE: Yukon Road

21st AOP PHOTOGRAPHERS' AWARDS

LANDSCAPE

SERIES

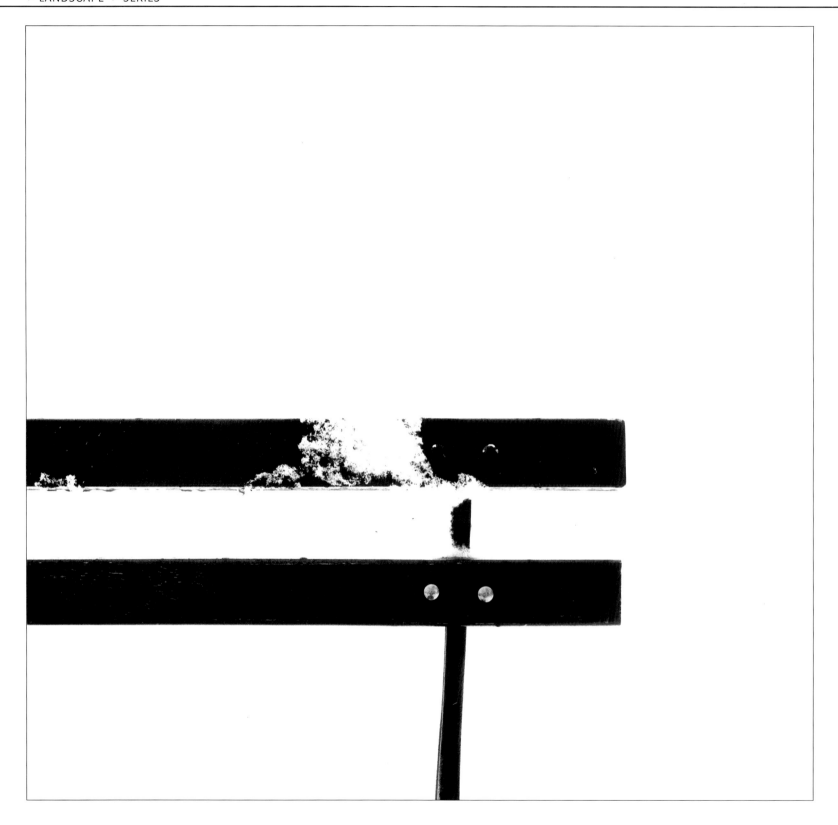

PETER DEFTY   MERIT

PRINTER: Ian Breckin at Silvertone   TITLE: Greenpoint, Brooklyn

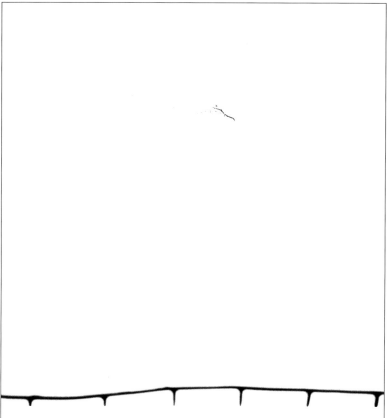

KIRAN MASTER   MERIT

PRINTER: Ian at The Print Room

ANDY GLASS

PRINTER: Rob Sara at Rapid Eye

ANDY SMITH

PRINTER: Andy Smith

TITLE: Goal Post 1, Goal Post 2
SYSTEM OPERATOR: Andy Smith

JAAP VLIEGENTHART

PRINTER: René Bierman at Souverein
CLIENT: Citroën
COMMISSIONED BY: Euro RSCG/BLRS

ART DIRECTOR:
Bert Kerkhof / Ivar van den Hove
SYSTEM OPERATOR:
Jan Stel / Fedde Souverein

Like you, we strongly believe in the beauty, impact and power of images. Digital imaging technology continues to gain momentum in complementing the benefits of classical silver halide photography.

Following the success of our large format Lambda digital photographic printing and Frontier digital pro mini-lab services in the last 3 years, with the continuing support from our clients, Genesis has now invested in providing CMYK colour proofing and Giclee folio print services in addition to our comprehensive range of digital imaging and traditional photographic services.

Genesis is proud to extend its continued support of the AOP awards.

Ken Sethi
Managing Director – Genesis Digital Imaging

STRUCTURES

SERIES

ALAN McFETRIDGE   SILVER

PRINTER: Charlie Fox   SYSTEM OPERATOR: Charlie Fox
TITLE: American Airport Series   LOCATION: Los Angeles

ALAN MAHON   **MERIT**

PRINTER: Alan Mahon   TITLE: Skeletal Buildings

ANDY SMITH

PRINTER: Andy Smith

MERIT

TITLE: Highway 1, Highway 2
SYSTEM OPERATOR: Andy Smith

TIM GOFFE

PRINTER: Tim Goffe

STILL LIFE

SINGLE

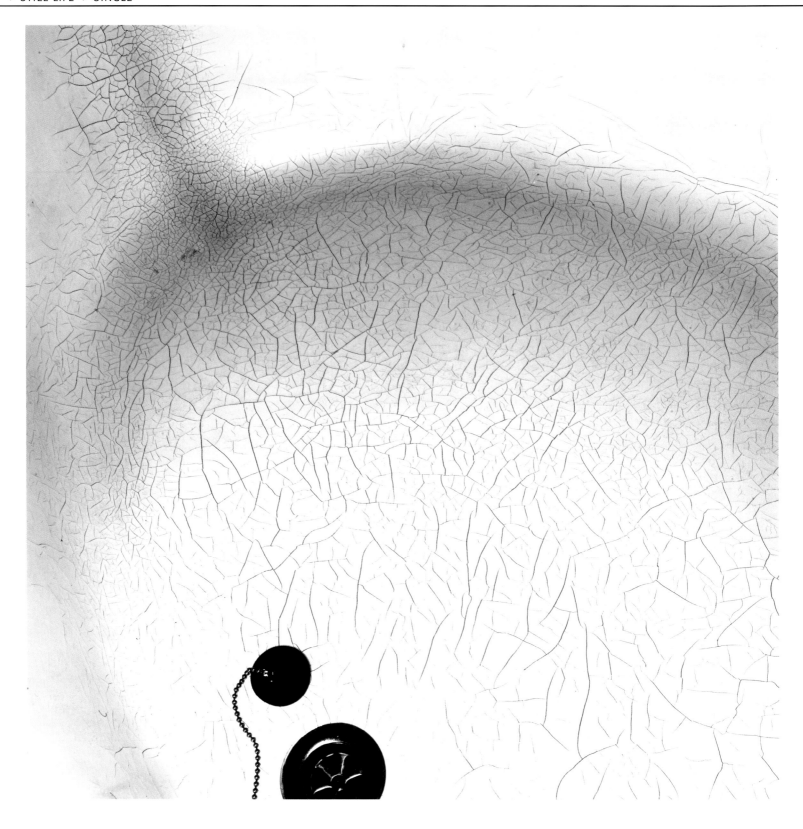

GUY FARROW   **MERIT**

PRINTER: Guy Farrow   TITLE: Hobi's Bath

KELVIN MURRAY

TITLE: Party Table

SPONSORED BY

CHUBB

Chubb Insurance Company of Europe is delighted to sponsor the Portfolio
category of the 21st AOP Photographers' Awards. Chubb has proven expertise
in insuring photographers and those in film and related industries. We have a
long-standing relationship with the Association of Photographers, offering
members comprehensive cover for cameras and other equipment, portfolios,
props, sets and wardrobe – plus employers and public liability.

Judith Isherwood
UK & Ireland Manager – Chubb Custom Market

PORTFOLIO

SUE PARKHILL   MERIT

As digital imaging continues to change the landscape of photography, the debate continues about how our industry will look in a few years' time. The cynics among us suggest that film will soon be cannibalised by digital, and cast aside completely in favour of more modern technologies.

At Kodak, we recognise that digital is here to stay – however, we do not believe that film and digital are mutually exclusive. We know that as professional photographers you expect the privilege of choice, and we are dedicated to giving you that choice by continuing to develop both film and digital products that will help you produce the highest quality work.

Whether you are shooting on film or digitally, whether you are using traditional printing methods or the newest and most innovative, you continue to produce photography that delights the viewer every time. Kodak is proud to support you through the Association of Photographers and the 2004 Awards.

Thank you to all participants for producing consistently outstanding photography.

John Culverhouse, Sales Director, Photofinishing, Kodak C&PI

PROJECT

HENRIK KNUDSEN   SILVER

CLIENT: Nokia
COMMISSIONED BY:
Julie Hughes at Grey Worldwide
ART DIRECTOR:
Nick Rowland and Stephen Godson

THEME: 'Something happened'.
Pictures depicting scenes where
something took place, perhaps a crime,
maybe something more innocent

BETSIE VAN DER MEER   SILVER

TITLE: Farm   PRINTER: Chris Ashman at Kustom

DAVID HARRIMAN   MERIT

PRINTERS: Darren Catlin, David
Harriman, Rob Sara, Jo Stout
TITLES: (1) Flint, Michigan;
(2) + (3) River Rouge, Michigan;

(4) Gary, Indiana; (5) + (6) River Rouge,
Michigan; (7) East Chicago, Indiana;
(8) Michigan City, Indiana

RICHARD KOLKER

PRINTER: Richard Kolker
TITLES: (1) Auschwitz – Birkenau. Rail spur to mainline at Oswiecim
(2) Remains of wooden barrack blocks
(3) Wooden barrack blocks, designed as stabling for 52 horses – used to house 1,000 prisoners

(4) Execution block for mothers and their babies
(5) Gate to gypsy compound
(6) Pond used for disposal of human ash
(7) Remains of crematorium
(8) Steps to underground undressing

I would like to take this opportunity to give a very big thank you to all our clients and wish them a prosperous 2004. The battle to win jobs has been fierce and I truly appreciate the passion and commitment you give to retaining control of the post production process. I hope to continue our team effort, bringing together our combined skills to achieve the highest standard of work possible.

Having worked closely with so many photographers, we recognise the effort, time and financial investment you have all made in submitting work to the awards. There have been so many memorable images over the years, some of which were never chosen. Therefore, it is my pleasure to sponsor the Judges' Choice section that shows off some of this year's great images that nearly got away!

Glen Taylor
Taylor James

JUDGES' CHOICE

ERNST FISCHER

SELECTED BY: Simon Norfolk   FROM: Landscape Series

ANDY GLASS

SELECTED BY: Desmond Burdon   FROM: Society Single

MARK KING

SELECTED BY: Alan Dye   FROM: Landscape Single

NICK MEEK

SELECTED BY: Suzanne Bisset   FROM: Society Series

TARA MOORE

SELECTED BY: Nadav Kander   FROM: Society Series

MIKE O'TOOLE

SELECTED BY: Nigel Clifton   FROM: Structures Series

BEN STOCKLEY

SELECTED BY: Sophie Batterbury   FROM: Project

Name	Telephone	Page
Stewart, David	020 7608 2437	50
Stock, Simon	020 7253 0868	58, 98
Stockley, Ben	020 7833 5878	158
Stratmann, Rainer c/o Steichen/Represents	49 172 670 7812 1 949 489 1938	66
Thandi, Kulbir	020 7403 0363	43
van der Meer, Betsie	07885 658606	138
Vliegenthart, Jaap	31 20411 7735	60, 70, 110
Wilson, Robert	020 7263 9901	17, 26
Yates, Mel	020 7359 9288 (Studio) 07973 377836 (Mobile)	27, 38

ZEITGEIST

Towards the end of 2003, three individuals from the creative industries were brought together to reflect on the wider trends and issues that have shaped and influenced the applied art that is commercial photography.

Selected broadly from the fields of advertising, editorial and design practice, they had an open brief – the only rule being that it was not a judgemental process of identifying 'the best', but rather an attempt to capture the spirit of the age – the Zeitgeist.

The AOP approached John Hegarty of BBH, David Stuart of The Partners and Marloes Krijnen of FOAM in Amsterdam. Working with design and advertising agencies and picture editors, a body of work was brought together that was considered significant, influential or otherwise noteworthy. This, together with work selected by the three 'curators' was the starting point for the process that created the following pages.

The three curators met together with Tim Flach, chair of the AOP Awards Committee; Jonathan Briggs, Head of Publications & Marketing at the AOP who was to put the images and philosophies together; Awards Manager Nicola Waterhouse; and AOP Managing Director, Rod Varley.

Photography: Eric Richmond

John Hegarty

John started in advertising as a junior Art Director at Benton and Bowles, London in 1965. He almost finished in advertising 18 months later, when they fired him. He joined a small Soho agency, John Collings & Partners, going places. They did – out of town.

In 1967, he joined the Cramer Saatchi consultancy which became Saatchi & Saatchi in 1970, where he was a founding shareholder. One year later, he was appointed Deputy Creative Director.

John left in 1973 to co-found TBWA, London as Creative Director. The agency was the first to be voted *Campaign*'s (the UK's leading advertising magazine) Agency of the Year in 1980.

He left in 1982 to start Bartle Bogle Hegarty. Four years later, in 1986, BBH was also voted *Campaign*'s Agency of the Year, and won the title once again in 1993. In addition, BBH became the Cannes Advertising Festival's very first Agency of the Year in 1993 by winning more awards than any other agency. It also won the title once more in 1994.

John is BBH's Worldwide Creative Director and Chairman.

Marloes LP Krijnen

Born: 22 Jan 1955, Amsterdam

1972-1980: Political sciences University of Amsterdam

1981-1984: Ministry of the environment International relations

1984-1989: Executive secretary Amsterdam Promotion foundation

1989-1998: Managing director World Press Photo

1998-2001: Director/owner Transworld agency for photographers

2001-present: Director, Foam Fotografiemuseum Amsterdam

David Stuart

David is a founding partner and a non-executive Director at The Partners, which has been voted the UK's no 1 creative design consultancy for the last 16 years. He has over 30 years' experience in design.

David's areas of expertise include creative collaboration and the use of wit in design. He was President of D&AD (the UK's foremost body for the advertising and design industry) in 2001.

David is also co-author of the design best seller, Œ A Smile in the Mind.

Photography: ©Martin Cameron

1. Marloes Krijnen, Rod Varley
2. Marloes Krijnen
3. Clockwise from front:
   Rod Varley, David Stuart,
   Tim Flach, Jonathan Briggs
4. Tim Flach
5. John Hegarty
6. David Stuart

Sch...you know it's not really her.

Sch ...you know who?

John Hegarty > We live increasingly in a visual culture. Overloaded with messages and ideas, spoilt for choice and hard to please. The art of communication is to grab attention with a distilled and thought-provoking message – one that captures the imagination and forces the viewer to react, hopefully in advertising's case, positively. Technology has made the craft of photography easier. Digital manipulation can save, help, correct, intensify a picture. The one thing, though, it can't do is put soul into a picture. And that's the one thing that, for me, separates good from great.

Great pictures talk to me because they have a point of view and aren't afraid of making a statement. They come from the heart. But above all, I ask the question, is it fresh? People overuse the word 'original' in our business. I'm suspicious of that word in both intent and reality. 'Fresh' is more honest and closer to the truth.

It would often be said that, in primitive cultures, people didn't like having their photograph taken. They felt it robbed them of their soul. Well, today the only way photographers can make a great picture is by putting a little bit of themselves into their pictures. If it doesn't touch the photographer, why should it touch me.

Maybe, after all, those primitive people were right.

Photographer: Alison Jackson
Creative Director: Robert Saville
Art Directors: Kim Gehrig, Caroline Pay
Advertising Agency: Mother ltd
Typographer: Ian Hutchins
Client: Coca-Cola GB

Art director: Grant Parker   Copywriter: Patrick McClelland   Art buyer: Sarah Pascoe   Photographer: Nadav Kander

The Ads > The first rule of advertising is to get noticed – because, as anyone will tell you, nobody bought something while they were asleep! What makes this selection of advertising pictures worthy of note is the broad range of emotions they plug into. Shock, charm, humour, irony, wit. Each picture has an understanding of its purpose, who it's talking to and why it's been constructed the way it has.

They capture a current zeitgeist. In each case, it's the picture that does the talking, that stops you and challenges your perceptions. And in virtually every case demands you go back and take a second look. More importantly, almost all the pictures belong to this moment in time. They reference a cultural event, a point of view, a moral standpoint. It is that that gives each image a greater potency and power.

Advertising by its nature is ephemeral – here today, gone tomorrow. And all the images function on the need to get immediate attention, but also have a depth that will leave a lasting and powerful impression.

Creating work that functions on more than one level is the ultimate challenge for any creative person. It is the thing that marks out good ideas from great ideas. What makes this selection great is 20 years from now, you'll be able to still appreciate the pictures and hopefully understand a little bit more the times we now live in.

Photographer: Trevor Ray Hart
Creative Director: Dave Droga
Art Director: Antony Nelson
Writer: Mike Sutherland
Advertising Agency: SAATCHI & SAATCHI
Typographer: Scott Silvey
Client: CLUB 18-30

John Hegarty >

'I found the work that resonated was the work that tried to reach out to me – the work that had humour and wit. I like the idea of the photographer and designer working together. Humour, I think, is a way of touching people. Making people smile is one of the most powerful things you do in communication, and not enough communicators understand this. We understand that seriousness is very important, and there are serious issues, but we need to surround ourselves with wit.'

Photographer: Trevor Ray Hart
Creative Director: Dave Droga
Art Director: Antony Nelson
Writer: Mike Sutherland
Advertising Agency: SAATCHI & SAATCHI
Typographer: Scott Silvey
Client: CLUB 18-30

www.club18-30.co.uk

(Below) CD: John C Jay, Sumiko Sato   AD/D: Nagi Noda/Motohiro Ando   AS: Hoon Kim   PHOTO: Shoji Uchida   CG operator: Hideki Minami PM: Kenji Yamamoto, Tatsuya Waki

(Below) Photographer: Nick Georgiou   Creative Director: Mark Roalfe   Creative Team: Mike Boles and Jerry Hollens   Advertising Agency: Rainey Kelly Campbell Roalfe/ Y&R
Typo: Lea Aldridge   Client: Anthony Bradbury

FREELANDER MAASAI **£14,995**

THE LAND ROVER EXPERIENCE   LAND-ROVER

(Below) Art directors: Feargal Balance, Nick Allsop, Dylan Harrison, Simon Veksner   Art Buyer: Sarah Pascoe   Photographer: Paul Murphy

www.volkswagen.co.uk

Small but tough. Polo.

Harvey Nichols Fashion Victims

Late night closing.

Wed/Thurs/Fri 8pm Knightsbridge.

Thurs/Fri/Sat 7pm Leeds.

Thurs 8pm Edinburgh and Birmingham.

Art directors: Ed Morris,
James Sinclair, Amber Casey,
Dan Hubert
Art buyer: Christine Saunders
Photographer: Drew Jarrett

a Harvey Nichols Fashion Victim

Late night closing.

Wed/Thurs/Fri 10-8pm Knightsbridge.

Thurs/Fri 10-7pm Leeds.   Thurs 10-8pm Birmingham.

Barry Stark. Died: Age 2 years.

WHEN Barry was repeatedly beaten from the age of two, a large part of him died. HIS hope and ability to love died. HIS future died. 38 years later, he put a shotgun in his mouth and died for real. WHAT a waste. AT Barnardo's we want to save children like Barry from a living death. WE combat the effects of domestic violence on children through counselling and help give them back their future and life. THIS takes time. THAT'S why Barnardo's works over the long term, helping over 50,000 children a year with nowhere else to turn. SOON, you'll read a story, in this paper, about someone just like Barry. "HOW sad", you'll say. THERE are thousands of children like Barry and they don't want your sympathy. THEY need your help. MAKE a donation. CALL 0845 844 0180 or visit www.barnardos.org.uk

Barnardo's GIVING CHILDREN BACK THEIR FUTURE

John Hegarty > 'It's very important to find a photographer who understands all the subtexts of all the messages, to know how to play with them but not over play them – knowing restraint.'

Photographer: Nadav Kander
Art director: Adrian Rossi
Copywriter: Alex Grieve
Client: Barnardos
Retoucher: Stuart Westcott, Lifeboat Matey

Jane Kent. Died: Age 3 years.

FROM the age of three, Jane was cruelly neglected and a large part of her died. HER hope and self-esteem died. HER future died. 19 years later, after being lured into prostitution, she was beaten so badly by her pimp she died for real. WHAT a waste. AT Barnardo's we want to save children like Jane from a living death. WE work with families, offering advice and counselling to give children back their future and life. ALL this takes time. THAT'S why Barnardo's works over the long term, helping 50,000 children a year who have nowhere else to turn. NEXT time you read a story like Jane's in this newspaper (and you will) you'll say, "this must never happen again". PLEASE, help us ensure it doesn't. MAKE a donation. CALL 0845 844 0180 or visit www.barnardos.org.uk

Barnardo's GIVING CHILDREN BACK THEIR FUTURE

Richard Fox. Died: Age 5 years.

AT the age of five, Richard's behaviour meant his teachers and parents gave up on him and a large part of him died. HIS hope died, his self-esteem died, his future died. 25 years later, after a life as an alcoholic, he fell into a canal one winter night and died for real. WHAT a waste. AT Barnardo's we want to save children like Richard from a living death. WE run schools with teachers who are expert in dealing with "problem children". ALL this takes time. THAT'S why Barnardo's works over the long term, helping 50,000 children a year who have nowhere else to turn. RICHARD'S isn't an original story. IN this paper, today, there will be similar. "WHAT'S the world coming to?", you think. DO something about it. MAKE a donation. CALL 0845 844 0180 or visit www.barnardos.org.uk

Barnardo's GIVING CHILDREN BACK THEIR FUTURE

e, I'm not a stalker
I was waiting for my wife.
I know it's hard to believe
But she's been in there for 6 hours

a Harvey Nichols Fashion Victim

I don't get married men anymore.
One man said it's because his wife is
taking all his money.

a Harvey Nichols Fashion Victim

David Stuart > 'Humanity and warmth is certainly a trend. This is reality. Companies are wanting constantly now to appear so much closer to their clients and their customers. We're all used to the veneers they put up in front of us. By approaching with this instant humanity, warmth and humour you're getting so much closer to those people – far quicker, they're not having to cut through so many skins of pretence or style.'

Art directors: Ed Morris,
James Sinclair, Amber Casey,
Dan Hubert
Art buyer: Christine Saunders
Photographer: Drew Jarrett

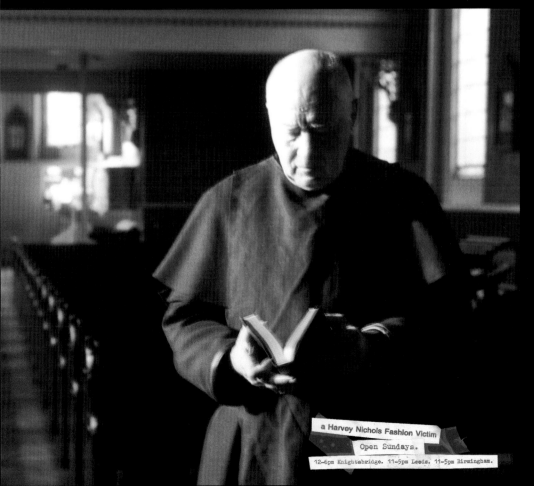

DESIGN

David Stuart > Photographers need feedback, hence the success of awards schemes. But this new AOP section is about evaluating photographs in their commercial context and asking how successfully they have been used to sell products, encourage investment, win trust, or whatever the objective may be. All the selected nominations are successful in these terms, keeping the clients happy and ensuring that thousands of people who come across their reports, stamps, brochures, and packages see something they are very used to seeing, but now... differently. Clever people.

While we were in mid-judgement, I happened to take down a book from the AOP shelves – a 1982 photo awards annual. The pages showed countless photographers who had achieved beauty and technical perfection. In the last 20 years or so, it seems to me we have come to desire greater truth and insight. In cinema terms, it's the equivalent of Dr Zhivago (big glossy vistas) versus The Full Monty (gritty, engaging); photographs are telling us much more than they did. They are more honest, more inquisitive, less contrived, more human and a lot more communicative.

Another thing: when judging these entries for AOP, the best ones seemed to have come about when a good photographer's portfolio had triggered a creative spark in the designer or art director. Our business – photography, design, communication generally – has been reliant on individual creativity for far too long. The majority of the selected entries here have benefited from collaboration – a sort of 1+1=3 effect. Working with others, sharing ideas, is invigorating and stimulating. It also produces exciting results.

ANNUAL REVIEW 2002/2003

fairbridge
Supporting Inner City Youth

(Above and right) Photography: Christine Donnier-Valentin   Client: Jennie Butterworth at Fairbridge   Design: Hat-trick design

Photography: Eric Richmond

Fairbridge is a charity that helps inner-city young people who have gone off the rails get back on them. The audience for this book is likely to be local authorities and support agencies that assist Fairbridge with funding and referrals. They need the reassurance of seeing a well-run, properly organised charity complete with efficient accounts and plans for the future. The photographer, Christine Donnier-Valentin, obviously worked closely with the designers, Hat-trick, and developed an intriguing before-and-after idea, showing the benefits of Fairbridge's help. These pictures reveal how informative and compelling photography can be. The review is an inexpensive 'documentary' in two colours; a great example of photographer and designer working within financial and production constraints for a critical audience.

The photographer and designer understood that this would be
'blocked' (like Warhol's Brillo packs) on shelf to create a multiple
presence in-store, but that it also had to work as a single pack
tumbling out of your chaotic kitchen cupboard. Consequently, the
image is nicely isolated, ensuring adjoining packs don't get a look
in. The beautiful infusing leaf photos promise taste-filled tea. It's a
very elegant, restrained solution.

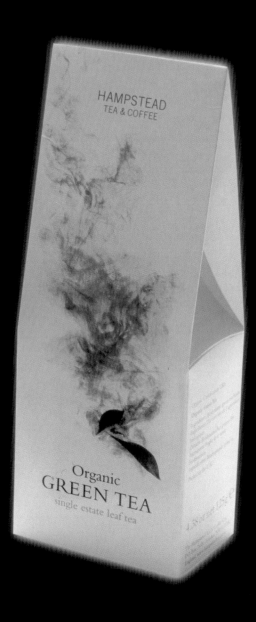

Mayday Living Brands   Designer: Barry Gillibrand   Typographer: Roger Akroyd   Photographer: Andy Seymour   Digital retouching: Ian Rippington
Client: Kiran Tawadey The Hampstead Tea & Coffee Co

This is totally different from all the others. It relies on a solitary image – a statuesque, high-key image of a naked woman. Its power is its erotic ghost-like appearance, coupled with its art gallery composition.

This photo doesn't explain, assist or communicate information. It leaves the purchaser of the music with intrigue and unresolved enquiry. It is this ambiguity which we found so powerful.

Photographer; John Ross   Design; Farrow Design, J Spaceman   Sculpture: Yoko II by Don Brown   courtesy of Sadie Coles HQ

Photography, Concept & Design: Anthon Beeke/Studio Anthon Beeke, Netherlands
Lithography & Duotone printing: Georges Charlier, Belgium
Two-colour printing: Freek Kuin, Netherlands
Copywriting: France Billand, France
Publisher: Papierfabrik Scheufelen, Remy Gass, Germany

This is a great job stemming from a very simple idea: our paper lasts beautifully — just like a beautiful woman.

The book is large format, duotone printed in black and grey, the only colour being three marker ribbons. On the left-hand page we have a shot of famous fashion models circa 1960 - 1970, on the right, their current portraits.

It is very confrontational. It demands you sit in judgement, agreeing with the lasting beauty premise... or disagreeing. Whichever way you decide, it's thought provoking and ensures a specific set of feelings have to pass through your brain. Brave client, brave photographer/designers: Anthon Beeke and Paulina Matusiak.

Brochures
and leaflets
how to
get the most
from MFI
Pick up our latest
brochures and price lists
here and take advantage
of our great deals
The products you can buy
The deals you can get
The services you can use
MFI Orpington 1st December 2002
MFI Annual Report 2002

Photographers: Matthew Stuart, Nick Turpin
Client: Ian Arnold, MFI Furniture Group Plc
Design advisor: Michael Wolff
Client partner: David Stocks, SAS
Designers: Gilmar Wendt, Tim Cole, SAS

The audience for an annual report are the usual suspects — city analysts, institutional investors, small investors, potential investors, and when they have all read it... staff.

If I were any one of these readers, after carefully checking the figures (at the back) I would flick through the rest of the report to make a snap judgement based on its appearance.

I would see candid photography of people, young families, enjoying choosing good-looking furniture in newly designed stores. I would certainly be surprised — this is not the MFI I once knew.

This report was designed and produced by SAS and uses engaging and honest photographs by Matthew Stuart and Nick Turpin. The back cover copy summarises it well: 'None were staged — what you see is what we found.' We liked this entry for its wit and warmth.

Photographers: Matthew Stuart, Nick Turpin
Client: Ian Arnold, MFI Furniture Group Plc
Design advisor: Michael Wolff
Client partner: David Stocks, SAS
Designers: Gilmar Wendt, Tim Cole, SAS

Photography: Richard Cooke
Art director: Jane Ryan
Client: Royal Mail

Everyone has 'ooohed and aahed' when peering from a plane window — aerial
pictures are enthralling. This collection of stamps showing Padstow, Broadstairs,
Portrush and other coastal locations has succeeded in bringing out the collector
in all of us. The arrangement and conjunction of the shots has also been carefully
considered — I know I'd be tempted to stick far more on my envelope than was
necessary.

    We chose these because photography had been used in such an unexpected
way on this take-it-for-granted item.

A publisher's interactive book list. This little book talks about books, lots of them, which 'view life from surprising new angles'. Westzone have published photographic books on gangsters, travel, concentration camps and T-shirts, to mention just a few.

The book list was designed by Rose Design, who have respected the powerful photographs they were given and created a format which demands the reader's involvement and enquiry. The design is as bold as their book's photography – that's why we chose it.

Art Director: Simon Elliott
Designer: Simon Elliott
Photographers: Malcolm Venville, Chris Steele-Perkins, Grant Delin, JocelynBain Hogg, Fabio Paleari, Sasa Felsbach, Itai Doron, Pepita Seth, David Corio, Guido Buffoni, Kent Klich
Printer/finisher: First Impression
Client: Westzone Publishing

The Firm
Jocelyn Bain Hogg

The Firm
Jocelyn Bain Hogg

Publication
February

Cover price
£40

Format
330mm x 265mm

Page extent
176

Photography
120 duotone

Cover
Hardcover

ISBN
1 90339H 28 1

Title
The Firm draws back the curtains on London's East End gangsters, the larger-than-life 'proper villains' who inspired recent blockbuster movies such as *Lock, Stock and Two Smoking Barrels* and *Snatch*.

From their nightclubs and strip-joints, to their boardrooms and bathrooms, these portraits of the underworld reflect the masonry of London's East End, where members are elected for their very particular prowess and skills. Old-fashioned rules apply: friends and family first, no swearing in front of the ladies, and, above all, never grass. This network extends across the country. It is about freedom and incarceration, loyalty and betrayal, violence and camaraderie.

But things are changing for the British gangster. Ex-KGB mafiosi are taking over areas such as prostitution, gambling and drugs, the surviving Kray confederates are writing their memoirs and making personal appearances at film premieres and book signings. The new breed like Dave Courtney are taking every opportunity to use the media for self-publicity, giving lectures across the country, writing autobiographies and film scripts.

These photographs capture every facet of the life of the modern villain from public appearances to mysterious 'disappearances': from members-only bare-knuckle fights to the astonishingly huge popular appeal of a Kray family funeral.

Author

EDITORIAL

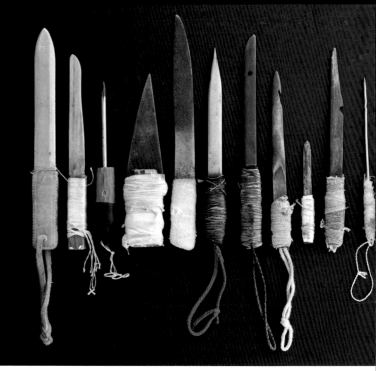

After a search in November 2001, prison authorities at Culiacán prison found the following items: 30 kitchen knives, 90 handmade knives (including the ones pictured above), 20 icepicks, 20 sharpened screwdrivers and four hammers

Marloes Krijnen > Capturing the Zeitgeist is about capturing a feeling. To see what is happening now, understand what has happened before and explore the possibilities for the future. It is also about the photography: the quality and craftsmanship of the picture, not the quality of the design or its advertising context.

What struck me was the convergence and exchange of visual language between editorial, fine art and advertising – for me this is the Zeitgeist. We saw editorial work that seemed located in a fine art sensibility that revealed individual creativity and a reflective process, and advertising work that was adopting the immediacy of photojournalism and the snapshot. Perhaps one reason for this is that,

Students of genocide used to say that Africa does not have the technology to kill hundreds and thousands of people *en masse*. In Rwanda, it took a few thousand machetes and a radio station. It was the radio that detailed the plans for the genocide, and the radio that reassured the participants that they were beyond the reach of international justice. And it did so without shame. Radio Rwanda's announcers sustained the pace of the atrocity, reminding listeners to keep on killing and stressing the special importance of eliminating children and pregnant women.

In Lukole, the radio is still an important propaganda tool. In the remote areas of northern Tanzania, reliable news of home is difficult to obtain and is subject to speculation and hearsay. To quell rumors and introduce an authoritative voice, Lukole opened its own radio station: Radio Kwizera. Though it broadcasts from Ngara, a town 27km northwest of the camp, Kwizera employs refugees as staff. Six years after the genocide in Rwanda, Kwizera is slowly persuading Lukole's Rwandan refugees that it is safe to go home.

I just arrived in the camp a week ago from Burundi. My mother stayed behind, so I am here alone. The person taking care of me bought me this cloth. I like it, the shapes are beautiful and the color is the same as my eyes.
Anonciata, 14

2

The army didn't have shoes that fit me.
I got three sizes too big – needed newspaper
and cotton to fill the void. Got these
titanium ones instead.

Al Holtz, 73, retired electrical engineer

How did it feel to win the war?
Like kissing a girl for the third time.

Sam Frackman, 82, retired traveling salesman

What are you scared of?
I'm scared of the outside because Rafael is there
and I don't want to see him.
But you are Rafael.
Now you understand what I'm scared of.

"Can you rehabilitate people back to normal life by locking them in the abnormal reality of a psychiatric hospital?" "Sometimes I think that the other patients or the doctors are making me sick. Madness is absorbed." Luis, 32

For Luis and other patients in Camaguey the problem with the hospital is not the medical staff (who are described as kind and at their disposal), nor is it the general living conditions, which aren't much different to those on the outside. The problem lies in the idea of a hospital closed off from the outside world, in the fact that they are excluded from real life. "One day when I was a child, my father came to the special school for retarded people and took me away, screaming that I would never learn anything there. That is the best memory of my childhood."

Today Ángel, 35, is out of the hospital. He is free to live in his own house, to work at the match factory and to go to the therapy centers around town. He is no longer just a sick person, but a human being.

Self-portrait by Ernesto, 49

today, editorial work – which includes photojournalism and documentary – has a different place in the information flow. If you have already seen the pictures on the BBC or CNN you don't need to see them again in a magazine, so editorial needs to go further into the detail and background, the whys and wherefores.

With editorial, whilst there has to be a good relationship between the photographer and the person who is editing, there is much more weight on the shoulders of the photographer: they work alone, they have a responsibility to the society they are recording and they have to make personal and political choices about the 'reality' they see and how to convey it.

Ghetto
Photographs: Adam Broomberg
& Oliver Chanarin
Design: Fernando Gutierrez
at Pentagram
Publisher: Trolley

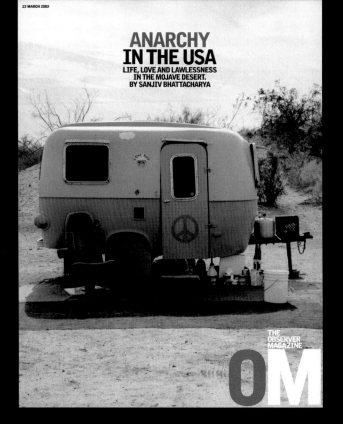

ANARCHY IN THE USA
LIFE, LOVE AND LAWLESSNESS IN THE MOJAVE DESERT.
BY SANJIV BHATTACHARYA

THE OBSERVER MAGAZINE

OM

Anarchy in the USA
Picture editor: Jennie Ricketts
Designer: Caroline McGivern
Photographer: Robert Yager

COVER STORY

LAND OF THE FREE

IN THE HEART OF THE MOJAVE DESERT, AMONG THE RUINS OF AN OLD ARMY TRAINING BASE, LIES A MAKESHIFT CAMP. THERE'S NO RUNNING WATER, NO ELECTRICITY AND NO SANITATION, BUT IT'S THE LAST PLACE IN AMERICA WHERE YOU CAN PARK YOUR TRAILER FOR NOTHING. SANJIV BHATTACHARYA MEETS THE DISENCHANTED WAR VETERANS, SOCIETY DROPOUTS AND SCRABBLE-PLAYING PENSIONERS WHO ARE PROUD TO CALL SLAB CITY HOME. PHOTOGRAPHS ROBERT YAGER

Painted landscape: one of the many garish sculptures which make up Salvation Mountain.
The work is the culmination of 18 years of labour by Slab City's resident artist, Leonard Knight

'I EXPECT YOU'VE SEEN THE UPTURNED CARS AND TYRES, RIGHT?' ASKS WILLARD, LOOKING UP FROM SCRABBLE LETTERS. 'THEY ARE INTERESTING CHARACTERS, BUT THIS IS UPTOWN SLAB CITY...'

Deep in the middle of the Mojave desert, on a slab of baking concrete, Jim and Rona slow dance to Perry Como's 'More Than You Know'. When the orchestra subsides, you can hear in the distance the muffled booms of warplanes bombing the nearby Chocolate Mountains. A murmur ripples through the assembled old folk at the Loners On Wheels afternoon dance – 'Hear that? They're bombing again. Second time this week' – and then the music starts up once more. A spot of shelling on a Tuesday afternoon is par for the course around these parts.

'That's nothing, you should have been here before the last war in 1991,' says Jim, giving Rona a twirl. He peers into the distance, lifts his chin and takes a deep breath, as though mingling nostalgia for Perry Como with the liberation of Kuwait. 'We didn't want for entertainment back then, you just stepped outside your RV [Recreational Vehicle] and enjoyed the light show. But that's Slab City – there's no electricity, but, hey, the fireworks are free!'

Slab City is the last free campsite in America – a litter of strewn trailers and Winnebagos in the wilderness of the southern California desert. For the last 40 years, up to 3,000 campers at a time have lived here without electricity, water, trash or sewage facilities. Some come out of poverty, trying to eke a life out of a dwindling pension, others to flee their tragic pasts or hide from the authorities. But many come for a characterful pitstop between the plush campsites of San Diego and Palm Springs.

Slab City has been described as either functioning anarchy, the antidote to the American dream, the last truly free patch of America, or a tragic indictment of the modern economy, a scree of human debris washed up by society. It may be all of these things. 'Post-apocalyptic,' is how some locals describe it. 'Like *Mad Max* 2003.'

In Slab City, toothless bums live on threadbare sofas alongside retired suburbanites in gleaming $300,000 motor homes, and together they watch illegal alien smugglers tear through the encampment with wailing patrol cars in pursuit. Turn a few quick corners, and you will pass in turn, a Rainbow Warrior, an ex-militia leader, a methamphetamine dealer and a gaggle of single pensioners playing cribbage. Drunks splash around in the Colorado river, while foragers return from the bombing fields with unexploded artillery clattering around in the back of their pickups. No one works. Stripped cars and rusted parts are scattered all over. Yet of Slab City's myriad eccentricities, it is the bombing of the Chocolate Mountains that in some way spawned it all. In fact, Slab City may be the only community which aerial bombardment has actually helped to create rather than annihilate.

During the Second World War, the US military selected this featureless patch of adobe and scrub to build the 640-acre Camp Dunlop Marine Training facility. Roughly 50 miles from Mexico and four miles from the tumbleweed town of Niland, the camp was sufficiently isolated for General Patton to practice desert manoeuvres and for the Enola Gay bombers to rehearse their nuclear missions ('post-apocalyptic' indeed).

When the war was won, the camp was dismantled and sold on, bit by bit. By 1961, all that remained were a few potholed mudtracks and the concrete foundations – the very slabs upon which Jim and Rona now dance.

RUSTY, 72, WAR VET, KOREAN

Above left: 'I like Bush. What I don't like is those Hollywood traitors who go over to the enemy and kissy-kissy. That's traitor Jane stuff. It's disgusting. Schools are getting dumbed down. Kids these days don't salute the flag properly. And that Ted Turner, he's buying up too much land down there in New Mexico. He's a real supporter of the UN, so I think they're trying to make some big closed preserves for future generations that no one can go on to.'

Clockwise, from top left: the Bill Clinton library; Loners on Wheels dance the day away; and a decorated truck

Squatters soon trickled in. Itinerant fruit-pickers from the north, hippies and many a war veteran – of Korea, Vietnam, even the Second World War – all of whom were attracted by the free parking and the clement winters. 'On my pension, free camping is about all I can afford,' sighs Ian, a 78-year old. 'It suits me because I've got arthritis, and Mexico's only an hour away, so I can get cheap medicines.' By the early 70s, a community of mobile homebodies had sprouted from the desert, 3,000 strong at its peak. Today, the population is just under a thousand.

'It sounds like a hard life, but it isn't really, for us desert rats!' says Jim, a retired building contractor who, at 67, has been a Slabber for over 15 years. 'You just need to conserve your water and your energy. I get my water delivered in a 50-gallon drum from Niland. I bathe in hot springs. I've got a TV, radio, laptop, and cellphone in my RV, and it all runs off solar panels on the roof. I suppose it's hard if you need your Starbucks every morning, but not if you like to hike instead.'

The likes of Jim and Rona make up 90 per cent of Slab City's population – known as Snowbirds, a migrant flock of RV-ers, they arrive from all corners of the country, but stay only for the winter. The typical Snowbird is an elderly loner who takes to the road after a late-life trauma, often divorce or the death of a partner.

Prompted by a spike of loneliness and boredom, and the sorry prospect of becoming burdens to their children, they set off boldly, like Jack Nicholson in *About Schmidt*, as much in flight from their pasts, as in search of adventure, independence and perhaps a companion to see them through. Jim and Rona met through Loners on Wheels, a nationwide network dedicated to the lonely RV-er.

The singles scene in Slab City is orderly to a fault – the RVs are huddled together into a kind of prim Singles District, an island of swept tidiness at stark odds to the chaos beyond. This gulf is a point of pride to many club members. 'I expect you've seen the upturned cars and tyres, right?' asked Willard, a retired journalist, looking up from his Scrabble letters. 'Don't get me wrong, they're interesting characters, but this is uptown Slab City, you're on snob hill right now, oh yes...'

Outside of the gentrification of the Scrabble set, Slab City begins to resemble the post-apocalypse for which it is known – ramshackle RVs, heaped tyres, gutted cars and the yaps and howls of skinny dogs. This is the world of the full-time Slabber, the year-long resident. Most fulltimers are dirt poor, with more fingers than teeth; they are frequently alcoholic, emphysemic and their raddled skin is cracked deep and dark. When the Snowbirds flee the heat in April, only 80 or so Slabbers remain to endure the punishing summers during which temperatures frequently rise to 130° in the shade. For the fulltimers, Slab City is about survival, not Scrabble.

'That heat will make your brains boil if you're not careful, so you have to cover yourself in wet sheets,' says Rusty, a hobbling veteran of the Korean war who turns 73 this year. Rusty lives down the road from the Loners On Wheels camp with a whining dog in a shack that might have been blown in from the hills. 'Every year someone dies of the heat in the summer,' he says, between hacking coughs.

For all its hardship, Slab City is Rusty's piece of the American dream. He regards his harsh but simple existence as a ▶

TONI, QUEEN OF SLAB CITY

'I'm the Queen of Slab City, didn't you know? Oh sure, they made me Queen because I got all the prettiest things and I been here so damn long. It's just me now, after my old man passed away a year ago. He was going fishing in the river there, drunk as usual, and 30 minutes later he was dead. Had an aneurysm. Dead before he hit the water. Boy was I mad at him for dying – I wanted him to live a long time so I could kill him a little bit every day. He got off easy. So I'm on the market for a man. That Pappy, he's got a sexy body, but boring as a box of hammers. Maybe Jay, he's another nudist. I reckon I could give Jay some.'

IF A SLABBER TAKES OFFENCE AT ANOTHER, HE'LL BURN HIS TRAILER OR ROB HIM. VIGILANTISM IS A WAY OF LIFE. A COUPLE OF YEARS AGO, A PERSISTENT THIEF WAS FOUND DECAPITATED IN THE RIVER

◀ tribute to the pioneers who built America and defined its freedoms. 'This is about as free as you're going to get,' he says. 'It used to be more free, before the government started trying to take our guns. If you ask me, they're betraying the people that made this country great. Us patriots were flying that flag way before 9/11. I ain't saying I'm a hero, I'm not. All the heroes are dead.'

Rusty is happiest talking about the war, the Second Amendment and the many attributes of Charlton Heston. He is less keen on the Snowbirds. 'They're *supposed* to be Americans,' he spits.

The animosity between the Snowbirds and the fulltimers is mutual, it has all the character of a smouldering class rift, the tension between the suburbs and the ghettos. At nights, on CB channel 23, Snowbirds grumble about the graveyard of car parts belonging to Tommy Flintstone, another Korean veteran and fulltimer. 'They say it's an eyesore, they say I'm ruining a pristine desert,' says Tommy, 'but these people have never seen a pristine desert in their damn lives! I tell them to stop chopping down the shade trees for firewood. They don't have to live here all summer.' Similarly, when Rusty used to operate a nine-man militia, here on the Slabs, the Snowbirds would call the cops. 'I had a militia for 15 years and we used to train here. But everyone got so bent out of shape when they heard the guns go off. I figured out a scenario where the terrorists could come over that hill and take over this whole camp by tomorrow. Who's going to stop them, a few sherrifs?'

As far gone as Rusty sounds, regarding an imminent invasion of al-Qaeda guerrillas, he is a model of sanity next to his neighbour, Gary. Known as Snakeman, Gary will coax a rattler out of your trailer, and take it back to his own, where he keeps a menagerie of serpents, scorpions and rats. His trailer is surrounded by wild dogs and his website, www.imperialvalleygateway.50megs.com, proclaims: 'I build animal cages. I enjoy junk collecting. I point rifles at other people and Im [sic] better than everybody else.' Rusty calls over, 'Hey, Snakeman!' But there is no answer. 'He's probably sleeping. You could go and knock on him, but those dogs will get a piece of you first.'

While the Snowbirds whine about the mess the fulltimers make, the fulltimers complain that the Snowbirds betray the spirit of the Slabs. Calling the police runs counter to the spirit of anarchy, of Slab justice, that prevails here. The Slab motto – 'If you don't like your neighbour, just move!' – is gloriously idealistic. Often, when one Slabber takes offence at another, he will burn down his trailer or rob him. Which is when a vigilantism rears its head. A couple of years ago, a persistent thief was found decapitated in the river.

Slabbers, Snowbird and otherwise, are proud of their tenacity, resourcefulness and simplicity. The example they often give, their mascot almost, is Leonard Knight, the 73-year-old artist eccentric who lives in his work just outside Slab City proper. No one else so embodies the bursting of life from its junk and dust.

Knight's Salvation Mountain is a monument of American folk art, hailed by congresswoman Barbara Boxer – who led the petition to have Salvation Mountain enshrined as such – as 'a unique and visionary sculpture encompassing five acres', an 'iridescent fusion of doves, clouds, flags, flowers, hearts, streams and Biblical messages'. Childishly rendered, in loud primary colours, it sprawls over the mountain, gallons of donated paint proclaiming to the heavens, 'Jesus I'm A Sinner Please Come Into My Heart'. Every day, pretty much, visitors from as far as Japan stop by to marvel at his 18-year labour.

WILLIE, 17, SLAB CITY'S ONLY TEEN

'The child protection people were messing with me and my mum up in Washington, so we came to the Slabs four years ago to get away from all that. My mum's mentally ill, so she gets a cheque and I take care of her. I quit school last year as the Mexican kids were beating me up. The truancy officer even said, "I don't blame you if you don't go back." There's a lot of prejudice against Slabbers, because we're poor. But we're rich in life. I've learnt a lot about survival here, how to get by without things. But it's a boring place. I just hang out here, go into town. Say, you wouldn't be heading that way, would you?'

Salvation Mountain is all the more remarkable for the pall of death that pervades Slab City. It is carried by the wind, the reek of dead fish which brim the surface of the nearby polluted Salton Sea. And, though it is rarely spoken, Slabbers will tell you that, yes, people come here to die, so as not to be found by their family. Death, they say, is common enough in the Slabs.

'I only want a companion before I check out,' shrugs Bernie, a fit 87-year-old from Lancashire via Vancouver. 'But I was married for 53 years, it's hard to be single all of a sudden. And people are cliquey. They don't talk to you if you're new. You'd have thought we'd be past that at our age.'

As the sun sets to a shimmering eyelid slice, and the vast jet-scored sky swirls with the finest shades of mauve, fires are lit all over the Singles quarter of Slab City, and old men sit around rubbing their hands and swapping tales. The CBs are tuned in, just in case there's a car chase, and almost everyone will be asleep by nine. Slab City awakes before most of us. By 4am, the Snowbirds will be off hiking again, Leonard will be up and painting, and the wild dogs will begin their yapping once more.

Given the impending emergency of uninsured elderly and demographics alone, Slab City ought to be growing, but the opposite is true. There are no Mexican Slabbers to prop the numbers – despite its proximity to the border, Slab City is a strictly Caucasian camp – and each year older residents die off. As for the younger generation of Slab City, they were moved out by the authorities last year, when child protection services ruled that Slab City was no place to raise kids. They withdrew 45 children and their parents from the camp, leaving behind only one teenager, a 17-year-old called Willie who looks after his mentally ill mother.

No one knows what will become of Slab City. The state of California periodically threatens to shut it down, but nothing ever happens – officially, the state seems to pretend Slab City doesn't exist. Rather than make the place an official campsite and charge a fee, as certain Snowbirds would like, Imperial County simply denies the Slabs a trash service.

'That's all we ask,' says Pastor Phil, who runs the Slab City Christian Centre. 'A trash service. We can't even dump in the local landfill, now that's not too much to ask.' After five years of evangelism and outreach work, Phil has become a first port of call for many desperate Slabbers – a soft touch for food, help with filling out forms, a trip to the hospital. Yet he draws the line at trash pickup. 'It would be nice if we had a community well, but other than that, there isn't any major problem here that you don't have in the average village in America, maybe even less.'

At which point Rusty comes staggering and wheezing across the yard. 'Pastor Phil,' he says breathlessly. 'I'm worried about Snakeman Gary. I haven't heard from him all day. I think one of his snakes finally got him. He's been bit about 15 times, maybe this time, I don't know... But I'm scared to go in there with all those rattlers and scorpions.'

Phil nods and excuses himself. 'OK, I think I've got the council's number.'

Just an average village in America. **OM**

TOMMY, WAR VET AND CAR DEALER

Above: 'This is the last place in California where you can do what you want without too much intervention from Big Whitey. I got one eye, four knee surgeries, four hip surgeries and two bullet holes in my shins, but I never claimed welfare. People on the dole, they get lazy. After two or three generations, they're professional welfare creeps. I don't need anything more than I got. I get a small pension and if I sell some car parts today, I'll go have a meal.'

Clockwise, from top left: Leonard Knight; his five-acre Salvation Mountain; and the Slab City Singles Club

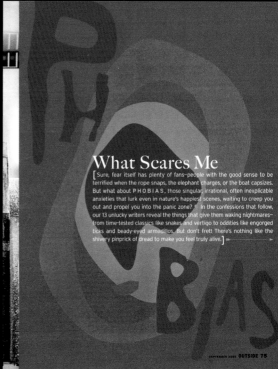

What Scares Me

[Sure, fear itself has plenty of fans-people with the good sense to be terrified when the rope snaps, the elephant charges, or the boat capsizes. But what about P H O B I A S, those singular, irrational, often inexplicable anxieties that lurk even in nature's happiest scenes, waiting to creep you out and propel you into the panic zone? ✳ In the confessions that follow, our 13 unlucky writers reveal the things that give them waking nightmares—from time-tested classics like snakes and vertigo to oddities like engorged ticks and beady-eyed armadillos. But don't fret! There's nothing like the shivery pinprick of dread to make you feel truly alive.]

Photographs by Chris Buck

(FEAR OF) FREEZING TO DEATH

First comes uncontrollable shaking, then a numb, frosty doom.

BY STEWART O'NAN

Because I was the goalie, when I fell through the ice it wasn't simple. My homemade foam rubber pads became two huge sponges. That it happened in a cemetery didn't help, or that I was at an age when I pointedly ignored things even if they could hurt me. We were there because we didn't fear death, nonchalantly tromping between the headstones and over the snowy hills into the far heart of the place and down into the bowl that held the pond. In summer, fat goldfish slid under the lily pads, but now it was solid—or so we thought.

I screamed before I realized I was standing on the bottom. The water barely came to my waist, I still needed help getting out, and then the wind hit my wet clothes and skin and I began to shiver.

I had to get inside and get dry, but first I had to take my skates off. The laces seemed tighter now that they were wet, and my fingers didn't work. A friend had to help. I didn't think to peel my wet tube socks off (cotton, worthless), just jammed on my Pumas and ran.

The running was uncool, and if I'd been out in the middle of nowhere it would have been dumb. Fortunately, my friend Smedley's house was only a couple blocks away, and I made it easily.

But in my worst nightmare, I don't. I'm out in the woods by myself. The shivering turns to even larger involuntary contractions as my body tries to create heat through muscle friction. I lose control of my hands. I stumble like a drunk, my speech slurred, muscles stiffening. The initial pain gives way to numbness. I get foggy and make poor decisions, like walking the wrong way or sitting down at the base of a tree and going to sleep. In the end, I pass out and die in the snow without a struggle, frozen solid, my skin hard as wood.

It didn't happen—it couldn't have—but I still have trouble walking on ponds, and forget about hauling a bobhouse out and then sitting in it waiting for a nibble. On shore, I can hear the ice creak, and know that someone's going in. Not me, I'll think. No way.

STEWART O'NAN'S LATEST NOVEL IS *WISH YOU WERE HERE*

(FEAR OF) SLEEPING BAGS

There's a reason they're called mummy sacks.

BY MICHAEL PERRY

On the whole, I love sleeping bags. When I got my first, a slippery orange thing lined with images of ducks and shotguns, I quickly discovered that no matter where I slept—the haymow, the back forty, the living room—I felt like I was lighting out for the territory. I took immediately to that snug, toasty, flannelly embryo feeling. You know the one: After a long day of hiking, you crawl in the bag and give out an involuntary little happy-shiver and hug yourself. And yet, a claustrophobic bugaboo lurks in the coziness. As a child, I once wound up head-down in my sleeping bag and went frantic, crazy ape bonkers trying to escape. Later, I slid from the top bunk in my orange bag,

panicked because I was unable to throw out my arms. Even now, I find myself opening the bag before I push my legs in, just to check for teensy wolverines hidden in the toe end. I think of bears arriving, and me unable to escape. Freud would draw conclusions based on the male preoccupation with issues of zippers and entrapment.

After years of cheapo bags, I treated myself to a military-issue mummy sack. "FOR EMERGENCY EXIT," read a tag sewn inside, "grasp each side of the opening above the slider and spread apart quickly, forcing the slider downward." Sweet reassurance for the claustrophobe. That night I slept in a farmhouse owned by a pair of photographers. Not wanting to muss the vintage quilts, I unrolled my new sleeping bag, slid in, zipped to chin level, hugged myself with the happy-shiver, and dozed off. It was July, and I woke up 15 minutes later drenched in sweat. Grasped each side of the opening above the slider and spread apart quickly. Nothing. The zipper was jammed. Be calm, I thought, and commenced thrashing on the bed like a prodigious eel. I jammed an arm out the face hole and, with one particularly contorted bounce, wrenched into a sitting position. Deep breath. Think. With one hand waving uselessly at the sky, I grabbed the interior zipper pull with the other. Bit down hard on the liner. Yanked and yanked. When the zipper finally gave way, cool air rushed across my skin.

Love your sleeping bag, I say, but do not trust it.

MICHAEL PERRY'S MEMOIR *POPULATION 485* WILL BE PUBLISHED THIS FALL BY HARPERCOLLINS.

(FEAR OF) SWIMMING

After one traumatic day at the pool, a lifelong dread.

BY JOHN UPDIKE

Hydrophobia names not only a fear but a disease—a generally fatal one, rabies, whose agonies of swallowing are stimulated by the sight of water; hence the name. Of course most phobias have at their root a fear of death, and my fear of water began, I believe, when my father, treading water in a swimming pool, invited me to jump from the tile edge into his arms; I did, and slipped from his grasp, and sank, and inhaled water for a few seconds. It felt, when I gasped, as if a fist had been shoved into my throat; I saw bubbles rising in front of my face as I sank down into a blue-green darkness.

Then my father seized me and lifted me back into the air. I coughed up water for some minutes, and my mother was very angry with my father for his mistake. Even then, it seems to me in the wavery watgo of this memory, I took my father's side; he was, after all, trying to teach me to swim, a paternal duty, and it was just bad luck, a second's slip-up, that in fact he delayed my learning for several decades. Part of our problem, that traumatic summer day, was that we had little experience of swimming pools; not only did we have no pool ourselves, but no one in our neighborhood or circle of acquaintance did, in that blue-collar Depression world. We were not country-club people. It is a mystery to me how we found ourselves at that particular pool, in bathing suits. Nor do I know exactly how old I was—small enough to be trusting but big enough to surprise my father with my sudden weight.

Henceforth I knew what it was like to look through a chain-link fence at a public pool, its seethe of naked bodies in the sunshine, and inhale its sharp scent of chlorine, but not to swim in one. At the local YMCA, the pool was a roofed-in monster whose chlorinated dragon-breath, amplified by the same acoustics that made voices echo, nearly asphyxiated me with fear. Aged twelve or thirteen now, I tried to immerse my face in the water as the instructor directed.

( )

Phobias
Photographer: Chris Buck
Publication: Outside Magazine
Creative Director: Hannah McCaughey

Prop Stylist: Sandra Swieder
Assistants: Nisha Sondhe and Brian Kerrigan
Associate Photography Editor: Quentin Nardi

Electrophobia

Tickophobia

but it was like sticking my hand into fire; nothing could override my knowledge that water was not my element and would kill me if it could. At college five years later, where one had to pass a swimming test to graduate, I managed a froggy backstroke the length of the pool, my face straining upward out of the water while a worried-looking instructor kept pace at the poolside with a pole for me to grab in case I started to sink. I think I did sink, once or twice, but eventually passed the test and stayed dry for years.

In the movies of my adolescence, Esther Williams smiled through the hateful element, using it to display her rotating body, but other movies glorifying our wartime navy, showed sinking ships and sputtering submarines. One of my nightmares was of being trapped belowdecks and needing to force myself through adamant darkness toward air and light. My lungs felt flooded at the thought; my hydrophobia extended to a fear of choking, of breathlessness. Life seemed a tight passageway, a slippery path between volumes of unbreathable earth and water.

And yet, graduating from college, I took the Coronia to England, and contemplated the ocean calmly from the height of the deck, and slept behind a sealed porthole. Adulthood strives to right the imbalances of childhood, and to soothe its terrors. My fear of water eased as, in my mid-twenties, I moved with my wife and children to a seaside town. Paternity itself, with its vicarious dip into the amniotic fluids, made me braver, and the salty buoyance and the shoreward push of seawater were marked improvements over perilously thin

fresh water. We bought a house by a saltwater creek in the marshes, and that was better yet; I plunged into our private piece of creek as if I were one with the grasses, the muddy banks, the drifting current, the overhead vapory clouds one with the water, my body mostly water. By middle age I had learned to swim and take pleasure in it, but still tended to float on my back, and to keep my face averted from the murky, suffocating depths beneath me.

OUTSIDE CORRESPONDENT JOHN UPDIKE WROTE ABOUT HIS GOLF GAME IN NOVEMBER 2001.

(FEAR OF) LIGHTNING

There's nothing like a bolt of lightning to put the fear of God in you.

BY KATIE ARNOLD

I have a deep, incapacitating fear of lightning. On occasions too numerous to count I've actually, involuntarily shrieked aloud at the terror of being struck down by a shimmering electric bolt from the sky.

The first such instance occurred the summer I was eight. My sister, grandmother, and I were alone at our cottage on a lake in Ontario. It's a great old wooden barn of a place, a hundred years old and drafty, surrounded by pines and junipers and blueberry bushes. It

bats roar out like demonic nuncios in a funnel of black terror.

And yet, I still cave. Because even though I fear bats, mine is an exquisitely nuanced phobia. It's not truly activated unless I'm in a cave and I see a bunch of bats, and then my pants catch on fire.

OUTSIDE CORRESPONDENT JACK HITT WROTE ABOUT TED TURNER IN DECEMBER 2001.

(FEAR OF) TICKS

They've come to suck your blood—and that's not the worst of it.

BY JANE SMILEY

Not too long ago, I picked an engorged tick up off the floor of my kitchen, thinking it was a stray chocolate chip. It only took a moment for me to see more clearly the minuscule legs and the hideous crease down the underside, but the idea that I had mistaken a tick for something edible freaked me out for days. Because now that I've had my middle mortality crisis and come to terms with just about every fear I used to have (and they were legion), the only one left is ticks.

I have dogs, the best of which is, unfortunately, a golden retriever. A golden retriever is a paradise for ticks—lots of hair to hide in. During

tick season here in California, sometimes we see two or three dark-brown ticks crawling around the top of the dog's head looking for a place to attach. That's repulsive enough, but it's the ones who found a spot, ate their fill, and dropped off that I worry about, lying there in the pattern of an oriental rug, waiting to be stepped on.

It's hard, if not impossible, to find anyone who defends ticks. Spiders and houseflies and rattlesnakes and killer bees and even maggots and leeches have their fans, who inform the rest of us about how useful, well adapted, or beautifully designed their preferred creature actually is—but the only thing you ever hear about ticks is that they carry Lyme disease. It is typical of the malevolence of ticks that the carrier is too small to notice until after she has delivered her insidious message.

Ticks seem to exist for themselves alone. They are ugly as nymphs and grossly disgusting as engorged adults. They live only to reproduce, which females do by dropping thousands of larvae and then dying. They don't take a meal and move on, like mosquitoes; they dangle by their mouths and get intimate. When feeding, they are motionless and passive. The worst thought when you find a tick in your hair is that it's been there awhile, that it drank your blood without your even realizing it. You have to ask, in the parade of extinctions, why can't we trade ticks for something we prefer, like black rhinos or snow leopards?

It happens to be summer now in California, too dry for ticks. I have some breathing room. I might even go for a walk one of these days. While I'm out there, I will visualize a world without ticks. It will be just like our world, only better.

JANE SMILEY IS THE PULITZER PRIZE-WINNING AUTHOR OF A THOUSAND ACRES AND HORSE HEAVEN.

Vivisepulturophobia

(FEAR OF) BEING BURIED ALIVE

A convincing case that it's the worst way to go.

BY DAVID RAKOFF

Vivisepulturophobia—the fear of being buried alive—is more sophisticated, more existentially bleak, than claustrophobia. It nullifies the most basic human egocentrism—that the universe gives a damn about our whereabouts. Rest assured: You will never be found, certainly not in this lifetime.

As a 15-year-old, camping near the Dead Sea, I blithely explored a series of caves, some natural, some clandestine cisterns carved out by Israelite zealots 2,000 years ago. More than two decades later, my throat closes up in panic at the memory of crawling on my stomach through lightless, birth-canal-narrow sandstone tunnels.

A cave is all well and good, but it still gives you room to flail, scream, and claw with bloody fingers on the rock walls. How much worse to be immobilized? Hemmed in by rock or sand—or even ice. Apparently, glaciologists in Norway have come up with a novel way to gather data: They carve tunnels into the core of a glacier using hot water, then climb through this frigid warren—hundreds and hundreds of feet down—amassing information. They have to work fast; in short order, the enormous pressure of the glacial mass overhead reduces each capacious passage to walkway to crawl space to eventually nothing at all.

Pressure is the force that separates the men from the boys, phobiawise. Think about the cumulative weight of that sand, earth, ice, what have you. It only starts with suffocation; the slow, inexorable squeezing of air from your lungs. Take it to the next level by contemplating the uncomfortable constriction of the thorax, the rush of blood out to the extremities, your hands and feet swollen and full to bursting. And what is that sound? Why, it's the groan of your pelvis buckling under. See it all clearly as your eyes emerge Marty Feldman-like from their sockets, the lids pried open like the gaps in a fat man's shirt. And there you are, marking each torment as it comes. A martyrdom too gruesome even for the most devout saints. But that's just me.

DAVID RAKOFF IS THE AUTHOR OF FRAUD, AN ESSAY COLLECTION. HE REPORTED ON NEW YORK IN SEPTEMBER 2001.

(FEAR OF) SNAKES

They lurk, they bite, they haunt your picnics forever.

BY JO ANN BEARD

It was the summer of 1972, rural Illinois. A picnic along the banks of the Mississippi. My friend Elizabeth and I, both 17, were forced to attend as a disciplinary measure. We were wearing gauzy peasant shirts and sullen expressions and were nursing stupendous, temple-clutching hangovers. The rest of my family bustled around lighting grills and slapping hamburger into patties. Elizabeth and I winced our way barefoot down to the water's edge to plunk stones into the current and say scathing things about my mother.

"She ought to try drinking a pint of lime vodka," Elizabeth said

darkly, "and see how it feels." Behind her, at head height, something shifted on the low-hanging branch of a desiccated tree.

One of the worst sounds a person can hear is the heavy thump of a big snake dropping to the ground at her feet. One of the worst sights? Same snake, churning around in a wide circle, opening its mouth to reveal a pale-white interior, vaguely plush, like upholstery.

Our loyalty to each other was such that we engaged in a brief but violent shoving match, cartoon characters trying to get through a doorway. The cottonmouth unfurled itself and wound past us—four feet long and stout as a man's wrist, but oddly flattened, like something molded out of clay and pressed into the ground. It slithered down the bank and into the river, lickety-split, like a strand of spaghetti pulled into a mouth.

Thirty years later, I experience startle responses not only to snakes but to lengths of rope, suspicious-looking sticks, and garden hoses, especially black ones draped over a fence or log. I am also spooked by snakish areas, including but not limited to grass, warm roads, stone walls, dirt paths, fields, old barns, sidewalks (trust me), tree branches, and, of course, water.

Being vigilant has worked pretty well, although not perfectly. Once I picked up a garden hose, after carefully making sure it actually was a garden hose, and there was a snake underneath. Elizabeth, on the other hand, recovered just fine and even went on to touch some kind of constrictor with a forefinger during a college biology class. Her profession was so sad we couldn't have seen a cottonmouth that day, too far north.

That's what my father said, too, when we came racing up to the picnic table, hysterical and shuddering.

"Oh, boy," he said agreeably. "Water snakes are big buggers. Scare a guy half to death."

My mother, squinting as she flipped the burgers, cigarette corked in her mouth, turned to consider us, green-gilled and sweaty.

"People who drink too much see snakes," she said.

JO ANN BEARD IS THE AUTHOR OF THE BOYS OF MY YOUTH, AN ESSAY COLLECTION.

(FEAR OF) STARS

There's nothing like the universe to make you feel puny and afraid.

BY MARY ROACH

Inside the city, the night sky is more or less a backdrop, benign and one-dimensional. It comes on predictably, like the streetlights, and I pretty much ignore it. There is the moon. Some planets. That spread-legged hunter who likes to show off his "belt."

Then I go backpacking. Without warning, the stars go thick as gnats and the blackness has ominous depth. You can see the other side of our galaxy. The sudden hugeness overhead unhinges me. I'll look up and practically drop my ramen. It's...The Universe. What frightens me, I think, is the abrupt, mind-slamming shift in scale. Like Alice after the "EAT ME" cake, I am instantly, alarmingly diminished—tiny to the point of disappearing. The longer I look up, the smaller and more vulnerable I feel, dwarfed by something huge and unknowable: God, the evil in men's hearts, infinity. I suppose, on some level, that the fear I feel is a fear of death, of insignificance and nonexistence. Or else I'm just a sissy.

Falling stars in particular unnerve me. Forces are at work out there, and they are not human. If there's that kind of weirdness in space, God only knows what's in the woods ten feet away. I spook easily in the wilderness, and I blame the stars.

MARY ROACH WRITES ABOUT CLAM FLATTERY, FRUTING, AND NEARLY DYING ON EVEREST. HER FEAR OF STARS FIRST SURFACED SEPTEMBER 2002.

EAST OF A NEW EDEN

BY ALBAN KAKULYA AND YANN MINGARD

TO DRAW A LINE NORTH to south on a map from the Baltic Sea to the Black Sea traces the European Union's unofficial border. It's not a concrete border, you won't find a wall its entire length, nor is it a recognised boundary but it functions as an effective economic corridor, separating rich member nations in the West from poor non-members in the East.

Seven countries that previously formed the buffer zone between the former USSR and Western Europe lie between the two seas: Estonia, Latvia, Lithuania, Poland, Slovakia, Hungary Romania, and, not forgetting, the Russian enclave of Kaliningrad. Each country has its own border patrols, often supplied with the latest thermovision and infra-red surveillance equipment, and

each is charged with controlling illegal immigration from the East.

Equipped with GPS devices photojournalists Alban Kakulya and Yann Mingard documented this often invisible barrier to the West by starting at opposite ends – its northern and southernmost points and travelling towards one another. Journeying by car, hovercraft, snowscooter or on foot they photographed the desolate landscapes which make up this contested line of divide as well as the people and the evidence of people (signs, border posts etc.) in a style closer to contemporary topographic pho-

tography than to classic reportage.

After six weeks travelling the pair met in a barren landscape of yellow grass at the point where Poland, Ukraine and Belarus intersect. On checking their GPS readings they found that they each had the same distance written on their screens: 860km – a total of 1600km between them. To mark the end of their journey they each took a picture at the same spot.

The compilation of images here goes a long way towards showing the beauty of these forbidden zones and the ambiguity of creating borders across the continuum of nature ◎

Borders
Photographers: Alban Kakulya and Yann Mingard
Art Direction/Design: Grant Scott/John Bowling
Agency: Strates/Panos Pictures
Publication: Foto8
Editor: Jon Levy

A BORDER INCIDENT by Ruth Fainlight

Gleaning olives, hard and black as droppings
or green as lizards, where they had fallen
below the trees and now lay hidden under
faded leaves (some leathery others sodden
from the autumn rains) or lodged between
thorny bushes on the stony ground —
an old Ligurian peasant woman,
gaunt faced like a gypsy sibyl, with
sun-stained skin and work-warped hands, clutched
her back, straightened up, smiled a greeting.

I was ignorant, and thought this border
territory seemed more archaic,
classical, than twentieth century, more
Italy than France; wished I could answer
in Etruscan or Roman Latin,
so smiled and muttered, *'Buon giorno'*.
From forty years ago I still recall
that look of furious insult as her gap-toothed
mouth spat out, *'Bonjour'*. An incident
which could have started a border war.

Zona: Siberian Prison Camps
Photography and text: Carl De Keyzer
Design: Martin Bell, Wai Hung Young
at Fruitmachine
Editer: Gigi Giannuzzi
Publisher: Trolley Ltd in 2003

A DAY IN THE LIFE OF CHERIE

Prime minister's wife, barrister, mother of four, charity worker – Cherie Blair certainly crams a lot into her life. But how does she do it? Barbara Ellen gains unprecedented access to the inner sanctum of No. 11 Downing Street and joins Britain's First Lady as she goes about a typical
Hodson

167

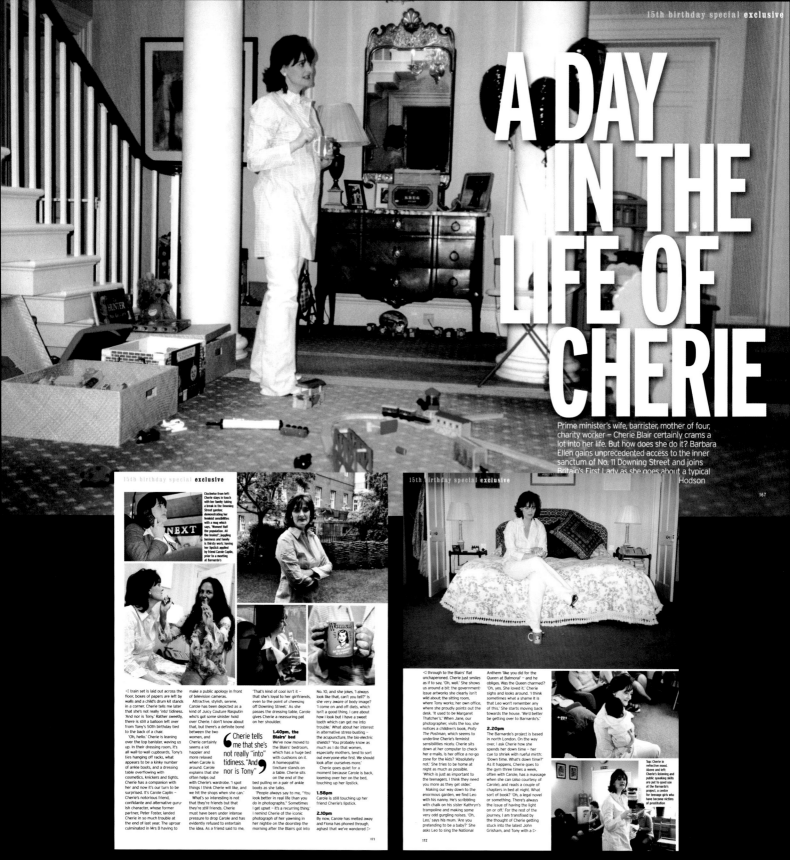

Clockwise from left: Cherie stays in touch with her family; taking a break in the Downing Street garden; demonstrating her feminist sensibilities with a mug which says, 'Women! Half the population. All the brains!'; juggling business and family is thirsty work; having her lipstick applied by friend Carole Caplin, prior to a meeting at Barnardo's

◁ train set is laid out across the floor, boxes of papers are left by walls and a child's drum kit stands in a corner. Cherie tells me later that she's not really 'into' tidiness. 'And nor is Tony.' Rather sweetly, there is still a balloon left over from Tony's 50th birthday tied to the back of a chair.

'Oh, hello.' Cherie is leaning over the top banister, waving us up. In their dressing room, it's all wall-to-wall cupboards, Tony's ties hanging off racks, what appears to be a kinky number of ankle boots, and a dressing table overflowing with cosmetics, knickers and tights. Cherie has a companion with her and now it's our turn to be surprised. It's Carole Caplin – Cherie's notorious friend, confidante and alternative guru-ish character, whose former partner, Peter Foster, landed Cherie in so much trouble at the end of last year. The uproar culminated in Mrs B having to make a public apology in front of television cameras.

Attractive, stylish, serene, Carole has been depicted as a kind of Juicy Couture Rasputin who's got some sinister hold over Cherie. I don't know about that, but there's a definite bond between the two women, and Cherie certainly seems a lot happier and more relaxed when Carole is around. Carole explains that she often helps out with Cherie's wardrobe. 'I spot things I think Cherie will like, and we hit the shops when she can.'

What's so interesting is not that they're friends but that they're still friends. Cherie must have been under intense pressure to drop Carole and has evidently refused to entertain the idea. As a friend said to me,

'That's kind of cool isn't it – that she's loyal to her girlfriends, even to the point of cheesing off Downing Street.' As she passes the dressing table, Carole gives Cherie a reassuring pat on her shoulder.

> Cherie tells me that she's not really "into" tidiness. "And nor is Tony"

1.40pm, the Blairs' bed
We've now moved to the Blairs' bedroom, which has a huge bed with cushions on it. A homeopathic tincture stands on a table. Cherie sits on the end of the bed pulling on a pair of ankle boots as she talks.

'People always say to me, "You look better in real life than you do in photographs." Sometimes I get upset – it's a recurring thing.' I remind Cherie of the iconic photograph of her yawning in her nightie on the doorstep the morning after the Blairs got into No. 10, and she jokes, 'I always look like that, can't you tell?' Is she very aware of body image? 'I come on and off diets, which isn't a good thing. I care about how I look but I have a sweet tooth which can get me into trouble.' What about her interest in alternative stress-busting – the acupuncture, the bio-electric shields? 'You probably know as much as I do that women, especially mothers, tend to sort out everyone else first. We should look after ourselves more.'

Cherie goes quiet for a moment because Carole is back, looming over her on the bed, touching up her lipstick.

1.58pm
Carole is still touching up her friend Cherie's lipstick.

2.10pm
By now, Carole has melted away and Fiona has phoned through, aghast that we've wandered

171

◁ through to the Blairs' flat unchaperoned. Cherie just smiles as if to say, 'Oh, well.' She shows us around a bit: the government-issue artworks she clearly isn't wild about; the sitting room, where Tony works; her own office, where she proudly points out the desk. 'It used to be Margaret Thatcher's.' When Jane, our photographer, visits the loo, she notices a children's book, Polly The Postman, which seems to underline Cherie's feminist sensibilities nicely. Cherie sits down at her computer to check her e-mails. Is her office a no-go zone for the kids? 'Absolutely not.' She tries to be home at night as much as possible. 'Which is just as important to the teenagers. I think they need you more as they get older.'

Making our way down to the enormous garden, we find Leo with his nanny. He's scribbling with chalk on his sister Kathryn's trampoline and making some very odd gurgling noises. 'Oh, Leo,' says his mum. 'Are you pretending to be a beast?' She asks Leo to sing the National

Anthem 'like you did for the Queen at Balmoral' – and he obliges. Was the Queen charmed? 'Oh, yes. She loved it.' Cherie sighs and looks around. 'I think sometimes what a shame it is that Leo won't remember any of this.' She starts moving back towards the house. 'We'd better be getting over to Barnardo's.'

2.20pm
The Barnardo's project is based in north London. On the way over, I ask Cherie how she spends her down time – her cue to shriek with rueful mirth: 'Down time. What's down time?' As it happens, Cherie goes to the gym three times a week, often with Carole, has a massage when she can (also courtesy of Carole), and reads a couple of chapters in bed at night. What sort of book? 'Oh, a legal novel or something. There's always the issue of having the light on or off.' For the rest of the journey, I am transfixed by the thought of Cherie getting stuck into the latest John Grisham, and Tony with a ▷

Top: Cherie in reflective mood. Above and left: Cherie's listening and public speaking skills are put to good use at the Barnardo's project, a centre for teenage girls who have become victims of prostitution

172

At midday on Thursday, 8 May, Cherie Blair sits in the modern, airy boardroom of the Matrix Chambers in London, quietly discussing client brochures with two of her colleagues. Not wanting to get in the way, I sit at the opposite end of the long table while Jane, the *Marie Claire* photographer, tries to snap away as unobtrusively as possible. Coffee is served, along with herbal tea for Cherie. 'Oh, thank you,' she says, taking large, grateful gulps as she flicks through the pages.

Marie Claire has been granted unprecedented access to Mrs Blair. We will shadow her throughout a typical working day and, hopefully, gain some insight into her public and private persona: Cherie the top barrister, Cherie the charity worker, Cherie the public speaker, Cherie the mother of four. And, of course, Cherie the prime minister's wife.

This is my first sight of Cherie in the flesh, and what they say is true – she is much softer and prettier in real life, with darting animal eyes, clear skin and glossy chestnut hair. Cherie has had more run-ins with the media than most, so perhaps it's understandable that she seemed slightly shrill and wary at first, her smile a bit too fixed, her voice a note too sharp as introductions were made. Now, though, Cherie seems to have come to terms with our alien presence. At one point, she looks over, smiling teasingly: 'You don't have to sit all the way down there, you know.'

Without waiting for our reply, she takes a sip of tea and bends back over her papers.

12.30pm, chambers
Cherie has completed all her business in chambers and we are driving back to Downing Street, with Fiona Millar, her aide, sitting behind us.

Hanging from the car door, there's a kind of Batphone, a hotline to Mrs Blair. The nanny has been after her, as has Euan, Cherie's eldest son. She reaches for the phone and starts dialling.

In this way, she is no different to any working mum I've ever seen. There's an almost palpable click as Cherie the barrister withdraws and Cherie the mother takes over.

12.40pm
Still en route to Downing Street. Cherie is belting out songs from *My Fair Lady*, *The Sound Of Music* and, at my request, *Jesus Christ Superstar*. 'I sing whenever I can,' she explains. 'My kids find me so embarrassing.' She tells us about a party where she performed a duet at a piano with Andrew Lloyd Webber. That's Andrew Lloyd Webber, the true-blue Tory, who once threatened to leave the country if Labour got elected and increased taxes as promised. Cherie grins mischievously. 'Maybe you shouldn't put that in.'

Is she a morning person? 'No, I need dynamite to get me out of bed.' Recently, three-year-old Leo has been having nightmares after being bitten by another child at playgroup some months ago, so Cherie has been spending a great deal of time in his bed. 'It's shaped like a Lamborghini. I'd never have got it if I'd known I'd be in it quite so much.' Is it always her who goes to Leo? 'Well, normally, I'd let him cry a bit, but it's important to let Tony get some sleep with all that's going on.'

Cherie's voice trails away as we arrive at Downing Street. We'd rather hoped that we were all going in, but Fiona tells us to come back later to have a quick look around the Blairs' flat and accompany Cherie to the Barnardo's project, where she is due that afternoon.

1.20pm, Downing Street
This time we're allowed in. Once through the legendary black door, and inside the main lobby, we are directed towards No. 11, where the Blairs famously opted to live because it was a better size for their family.

Suddenly, magically, we are standing in the Blairs' personal living space. Their main den area is definitely 'lived in'. The first things you notice are the piano and the *Gone With The Wind* staircase, which has a baby gate bolted onto the banisters. Toys are scattered everywhere, a ▷

168

Clockwise from above: Cherie dons her trainers for a visit to the gym; the Blairs' main living space, scattered with toys; leaving Downing Street through the legendary black door; ready for business in a smart suit; meeting with colleagues at Matrix Chambers

A Day in the life of Cherie
Photographer: Jane Hodson
Client: British Marie Claire
(editor Marie O'Riordan)
Creative director: Stuart Selner
Picture editor: Luisa Nitrato-Izzo
Commissioning editor: Vanessa Thompson

◁ pillow over his face, grumbling about how he can't get to sleep.

2.50pm, Barnardo's project
We arrive at the Barnardo's project, which houses and supports teenage girls who have become victims of prostitution, either through homelessness or drugs. Cherie has been president of Barnardo's for several years now, and spends a significant amount of time helping to publicise the various projects. Cynthia, the Barnardo's organiser, clearly thinks she's a godsend. 'It's so difficult to get funding, and it's such a boost to have her visit.' She greets Cherie warmly and escorts her into the sitting room.

Whatever the young women were expecting the PM's wife to be like (formal, reserved, scary?), it doesn't happen. Cherie plonks herself down in the middle of the group, and starts chatting, laughing, advising and asking for their stories. Maybe it's the legal training kicking in, but she is a good listener. Some of the girls are very funny and spirited, others are painfully introverted. One has a baby with her, another has one on the way. The latter gives a vivid description of how Barnardo's has helped: 'I felt like a fizzy drink being shaken and shaken. This place stops you fizzing over.'

It transpires that this girl has managed to cut down her smoking, from 80 a day to twenty. (It's quite amusing watching Cherie trying to handle that one tactfully.) As well as being president of Barnardo's, Cherie supports a number of other charities, including Refuge, Breast Cancer Care, SCOPE, Sargent Cancer Care For Children and Victim Support. Going by her performance today, they're very lucky to have her.

At a signal from Cynthia, we leave to allow the young women at the centre some private time with Cherie.

6.45pm
We're back at Downing Street waiting for Cherie. For her final engagement of the day, she is

174

to attend the Asian Women of Achievement Awards at the Park Lane Hilton Hotel and will present one of the gongs.

Cherie told us earlier that she'd had a sari specially made, the cut slightly altered because she had no intention of flashing her midriff. Finally, she appears in her sparkly gold number, swishing through Downing Street's offices, past the office workers, desks, computers and fax machines, looking like a cross between a goddess and an office temp. Once in the car, she talks enthusiastically about the Barnardo's visit. 'The girls were just great, weren't they?'

7.15pm, Park Lane Hilton Hotel
Arriving at the Park Lane Hilton, the press are waiting to catch Cherie in her sari. As soon as she has one foot out of the car, she is engulfed by flashbulbs. Once past that, she is surrounded by organisers and well-wishers. Upstairs in the VIP room, I watch Cherie Blair from a distance, wondering if her whole life is about being swallowed alive.

> "Down time, what down time?" she shrieks with rueful mirth

That said, she looks happy enough, laughing, talking, greeting, being greeted, ignoring the trays of champagne, clutching her glass of orange juice.

The last time I see Cherie Blair, it's fairly late in the evening. The dinner is over, Cherie has said a few words and presented the gong, and is now preparing to leave. It's been a long day. I'm a bit squiffy on champagne, so I just want to say goodbye and how it was nice to meet her, all that kind of thing. 'Yes,' says Cherie, adding in a sad-amused way: 'I do hope I'm not going to be too angry with you when this comes out.' Before I can reply, there's a quick rustle of indian silk and the pitter-patter of jewelled slippers.

Cherie Blair, mother of four, barrister, charity worker, public speaker and thoroughly modern Ms, has left the building ∎
For more details on Barnardo's or to make a donation, call 020-8550 8822 or visit www.barnardos.org.uk.

Clockwise from top: on her way to the Asian Women of Achievement Awards, wearing a sparkly gold sari specially made for the occasion; Cherie shows off her sari to office workers in Downing Street; meeting and greeting with the Aga Khan's wife, on Cherie's left; presenting a gong to the neuroscientist Professor Faraneh Vargha-Khadem; heading home at the end of the day

FUJIFILM

Professional

Fujifilm Professional has always been proud to associate itself with the AOP and, in particular, has always taken a keen interest in the fortunes of those coming into photography – initially as students and then as assistant photographers. Although we are all aware of the changing technologies available to photographers, the key attributes of the successful photographer will always revolve around the traditional skills associated with composition and light, irrespective of the capture medium. Fujifilm remains committed to professional photography, appropriately illustrated by the introduction during 2003 of three new professional film emulsions.

THE JUDGES

< Anderson & Low >

Jonathan Anderson and Edwin Low have been collaborating as the team 'Anderson & Low' since 1990. After the Royal Academy of Arts exhibited one of their early collaborations, they decided to embark upon a long-term partnership which continues to this day. Their fine art work includes portraiture, nudes, architectural studies, reportage, landscape and highly disciplined studio-based images. Works by Anderson & Low, all noted for meticulous attention to form, lighting and printing, have been exhibited world-wide and is in a number of permanent collections, including the National Portrait Gallery of both the UK and Australia, and the United States Olympic Committee,

Their major exhibition The Athlete was staged at the invitation of the National Art Gallery of Malaysia for the 1998 Commonwealth Games Cultural Festival. It has been on tour internationally for the last four years, with venues including the US Olympic Centre and the National Portrait Gallery of Australia for the 2000 Olympic Games. Following the success of that exhibition, Anderson & Low were asked by the US Olympic Committee to photograph a new project, American Athletes, which was exhibited at the US Olympic Centre in 2001 and toured through the USA.

Anderson & Low have been the proud recipients of one Gold and two Silver

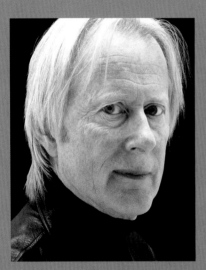

< Nigel Rose

Nigel got into advertising in the late 1960s at Leo Burnett. He then joined Collet Dickinson & Pearce in 1975. There he created campaigns for Clarks shoes, Mary Quant cosmetics and the award-winning Benson & Hedges surreal cigarette posters. From 1992 there followed a brief stint at TBWA as creative director where he created the famous HELLO BOYS Wonderbra campaign. He joined Euro RSCG Wnek Gosper in 1994 as head of art, partnering Mark Wnek. At Euro he created work for the Butter Council, Peugeot, Credit Suisse, The Museum of London, Abbey National

< Joanne Smith

Joanne Smith is a Design Director at leading UK brand design consultancy Lewis Moberly. She studied graphic design at Newcastle Upon Tyne, joining Lewis Moberly as a graduate in 1988. Joanne has worked on major design projects for brands such as Remy Martin, Jaeger, Bollinger, Johnson and Johnson and Boots. Her award-winning work includes the Pol Roger portfolio, Ferreria Anniversary Port, Finca Flichman wines and Waitrose Canned Fruits.

Joanne is a member of British Design and Art Direction and judged

David Gardiner >

David Gardiner is a London-based photographer's agent, representing some of the UK's leading photographers. He currently represents Richard Mummery, Nick Georghiou, Mooney Photo, James Day, Brian Stewart and Dod Miller. David Gardiner has been an associate member of the AOP since 1983.

Sung Ma >

Graduated from the popular breeding ground of photographers that is Blackpool College of Art. My main areas of interest are portrature and fashion although lately I am finding still life more and more appealing. Aside from photography, my other passion is travelling and football. On the former... i 've rececntly had the opportunity to undertake a trip to the Far East. I've been a few times but it's still an eye opener with every trip; and on the latter... well, I would give my right arm for the Foxes to stay up in the premiership.

Tabitha Wilson >

Tabitha Wilson; Art Director, Photonica, co-ordinating, producing and directing photographic projects.
A graduate from Winchester School of Art '97, she worked with the Contemporary Art Society on various commissions, specialist and corporate collections then joined the Photonica photo agency in the beginning of 1998. Photonica continues to be a leader in high-end rights-managed photography, producing energetic, emotional and conceptually driven imagery and remains a key source for new ideas in creative contemporary photography.

FUJIFILM
Professional

ASSISTANTS' AWARDS

SPONSORED BY

LIFESTYLE & PORTRAITURE

SINGLE

RIK BRAUNE   **WINNER**

PRINTER: René Bierman at Souverein   SYSTEM OPERATOR: Hans Berghuis at
TITLE: Joop   Souverein

SAMUEL HICKS   **WINNER**

PRINTER: Pat Cline at Genesis   TITLE: Itsuma

JON DAY   MERIT

PRINTER: Charly at Outback Printworks   TITLE: Bermondsey BMX Boys

PHIL MILLS   **MERIT**

PRINTER: Gil at Goldenshot

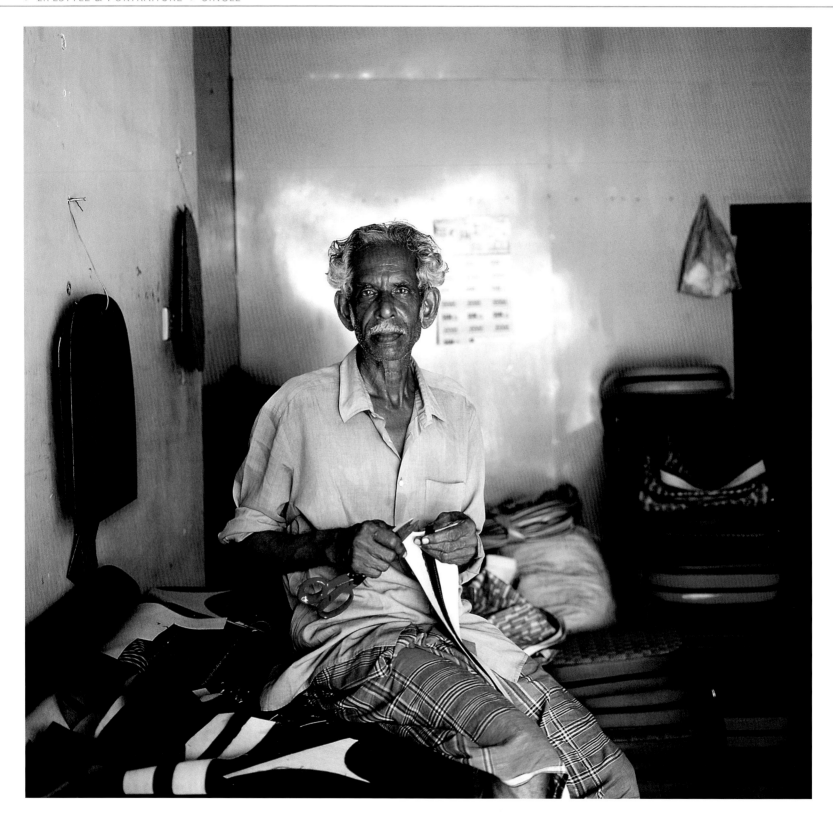

JESSE STAGG   MERIT

PRINTER: Jesse Stagg   TITLE: Cushion maker – Sri Lanka

MEREDITH ANDREWS

PRINTER: Mark Foxwell   TITLE: Baseball Player, Havana

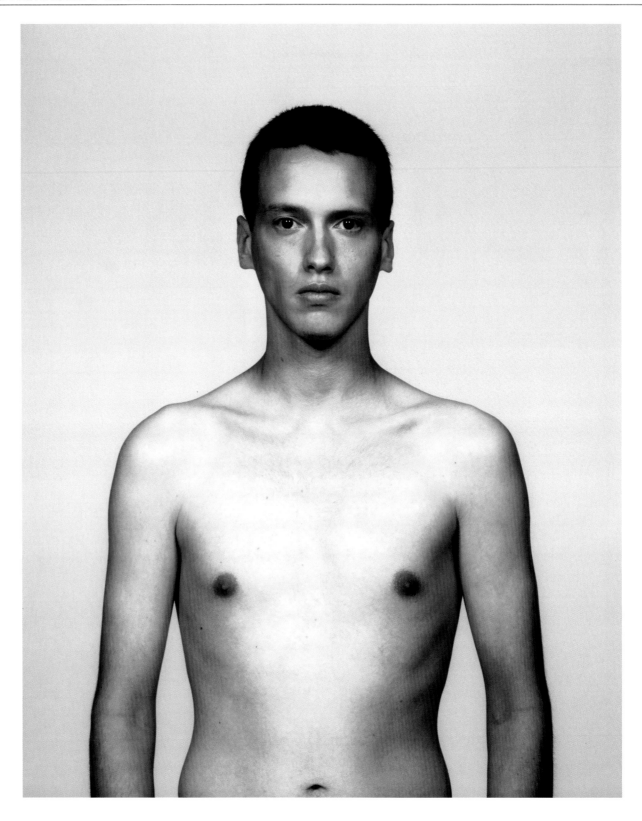

MATTHEW FARRANT

TITLE: John

LYDIA GOLDBLATT

PRINTER: Lee Adams at Metro

SAMUEL HICKS

PRINTER: Robin Bell

HANNAH MENTZ

PRINTER: Richard Miller, Ceta Imaging   TITLE: Brighton Boy

JOEL REDMAN

TITLE: Alfie   STYLIST: Jaine Bevan

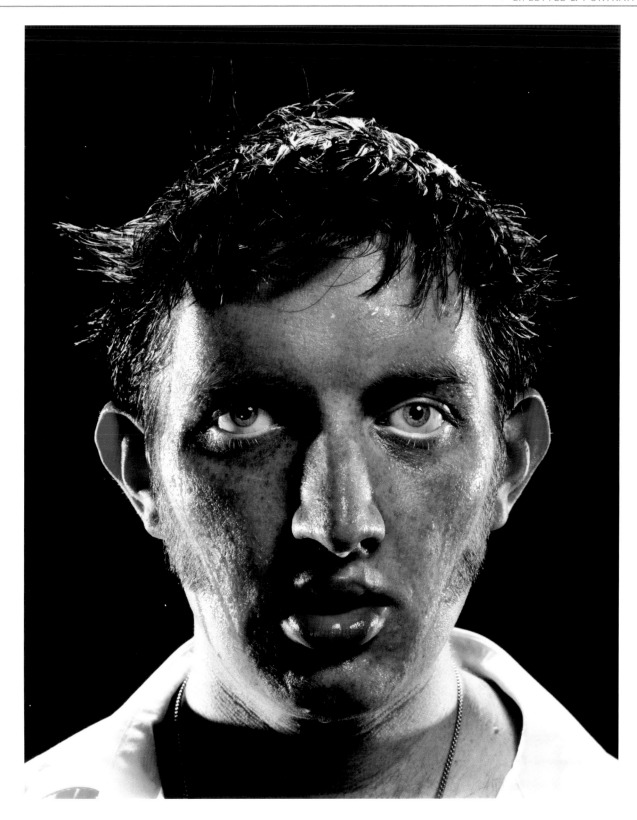

GRAEME STUART

PRINTER: Graeme Stuart   TITLE: Brian P Campbell

GREG WHITE

ASSISTANTS'
AWARDS

SPONSORED BY

LIFESTYLE & PORTRAITURE

SERIES

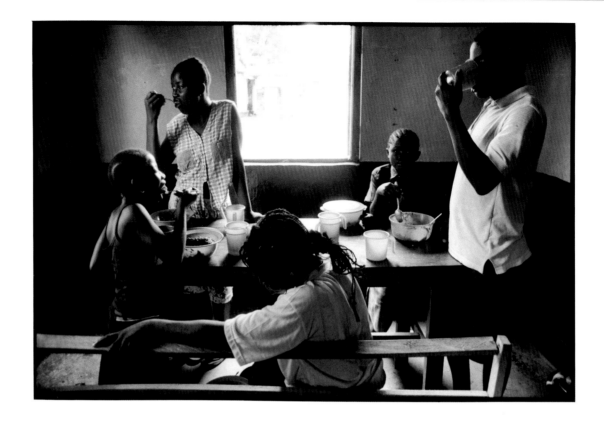

CAROLINE IRBY   MERIT

PRINTER: Keith Barratt at Metro
TITLES: (1) Lunch time at IRC home
for ex-child soldiers awaiting
reunification with their families,
Yengema, Sierra Leone.

(2) 11-year-old former child soldiers
return to school, Makeni, Sierra Leone

(3) Its been four years since I touched a football. Joseph, 12, ex-child soldier, Freetown, Sierra Leone

(4) Children at a school reintegration programme for ex-combattants, Makeni, Sierra Leone

DAVE BENTLEY

PRINTER: Dave Bentley   TITLE: Colours

SAMUEL HICKS

SYSTEM OPERATOR:
Dan Tierne at The Dairy Studio
PRINTER: Ian Brearey at Genesis
PRODUCED BY:
Caroline Flint & Stuart Hunt

ASSISTANT: David Denny
LIGHTING SUPPLIED BY:
Cine Build Ltd and the Pro Centre
TITLE: Itsuma Tanaka and
Stuart Gibson Kendo Players

SPENCER MURPHY

PRINTER: Chris Ashman at Metro   TITLE: Relative

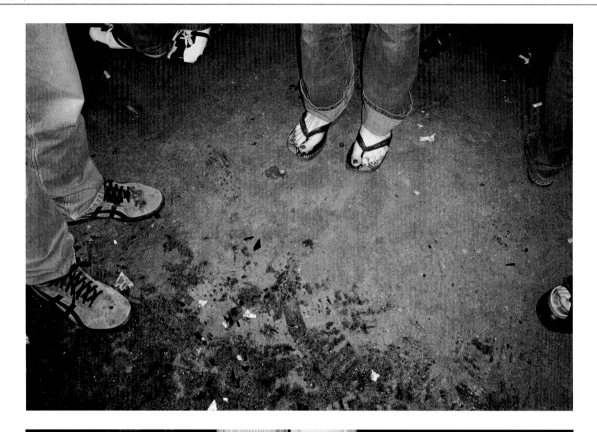

ANDY RIGBY

PRINTER: ANDY RIGBY

SPONSORED BY

FASHION
& BEAUTY

SINGLE

SAM CHRISTMAS

PRINTER: Sam Christmas   STYLING: Charlotte Williams

JOEL REDMAN

TITLE: Gem

SPONSORED BY

FASHION & BEAUTY

SERIES

JOEL MICAH MILLER   **WINNER**

PRINTER: Joel Micah Miller
TITLES: (1) The Sleeping Czar's
Daughter / Russian Fairytales

(2) The Snow Maiden / Russian Fairytales
(3) The Two Sisters / Russian Fairytales
(4) The Mistress of Copper Mountain /
Russian Fairytales

Fujifilm Assistants' Awards

SAM CHRISTMAS   MERIT

PRINTER: Sam Christmas   STYLING: Charlotte Williams
                                          MAKE-UP: Sian Chang

MATTHEW BRODIE

PRINTER: Matthew Brodie   MAKE-UP: Jaimee Thomas

SAM CHRISTMAS

PRINTER: Sam Christmas

Fujifilm Assistants' Awards

EMMA MITCHELL

PRINTER: Emma Mitchell
OTHER: Thank you Ellie

MARK WINKLEY

TITLE: Last Rites
CLIENT: Flux Magazine
ART DIRECTOR: Dominic Thomas

STYLING: Lindsay Garvin
HAIR & MAKE-UP: Amanda Bowen
MODELS: Abbie at MMA & Alison
Canavan at M+P

SPONSORED BY

LANDSCAPES, INTERIORS & EXTERIORS

SINGLE

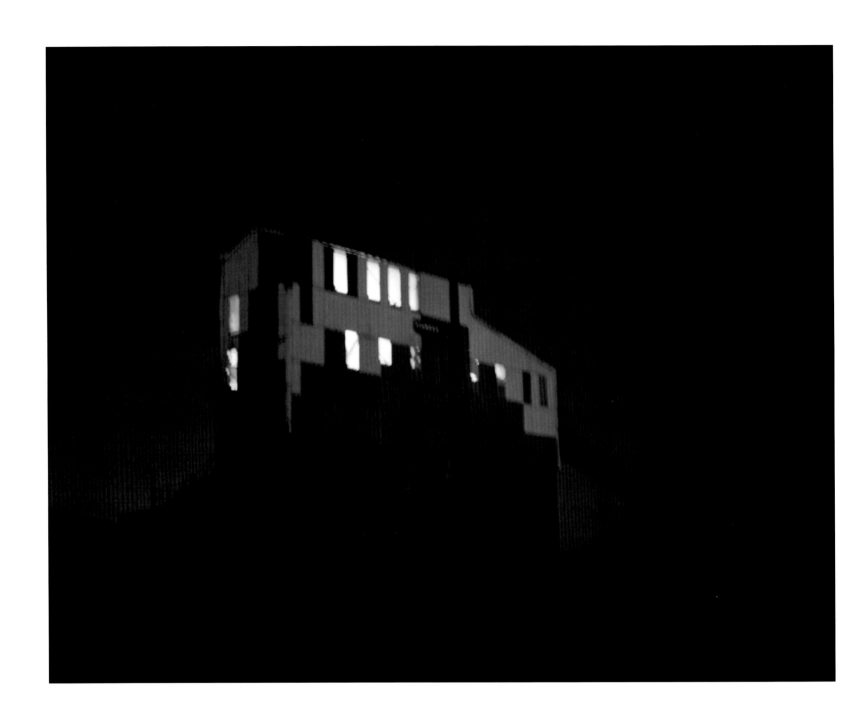

DAVID DENNY   WINNER

PRINTER: David Denny

SORAYA SCHOFIELD   **MERIT**

PRINTER: Soraya Schofield   TITLE: End of the Passageway

ARMANDO A D FERRARI

PRINTER: A Ferrari   TITLE: Monument #9
                                       COMPANY: Twobobrocket

SAMUEL HICKS

PRINTER: Pat Cline at Genesis

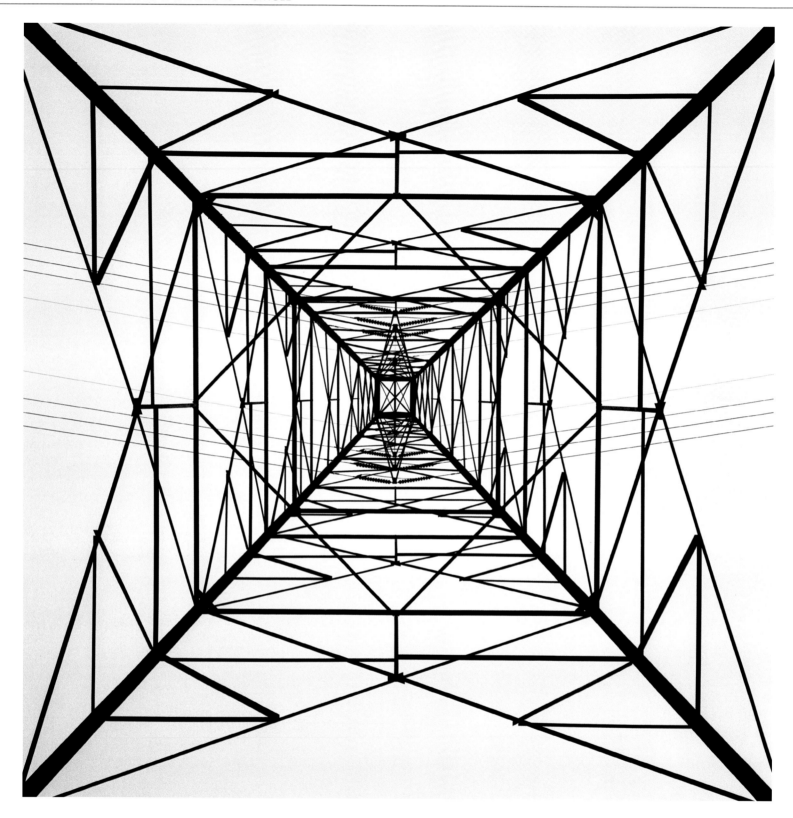

ROGER RICHARDS

PRINTER: Roger Richards

GREG WHITE

SPONSORED BY

LANDSCAPES, INTERIORS & EXTERIORS

SERIES

PEDRO ALVAREZ　　　　　**WINNER**

PRINTER: Pedro Alvarez

Fujifilm Assistants' Awards

SPENCER MURPHY   **WINNER**

PRINTER: Chris Ashman at Metro

NICKY WALSH

PRINTER: Nicky Walsh   TITLE: Bingo Hall

SPONSORED BY

STILL LIFE

SINGLE

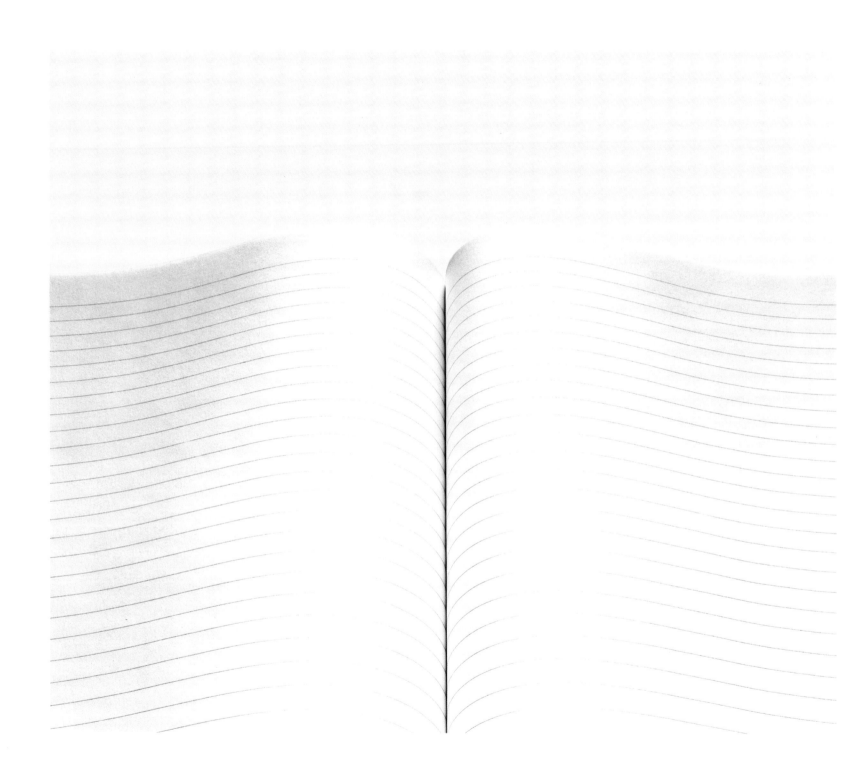

NICHOLAS BARTLE

PRINTER: Nicholas Bartle   TITLE: Paper

SIMONE KOCH

PRINTER:
Chris Ellison at Metro Imaging

ANDY STEWART

PRINTER: Steve Barnes   TITLE: Shoes

Fujifilm Assistants' Awards

ASSISTANTS' AWARDS

STILL LIFE

SERIES

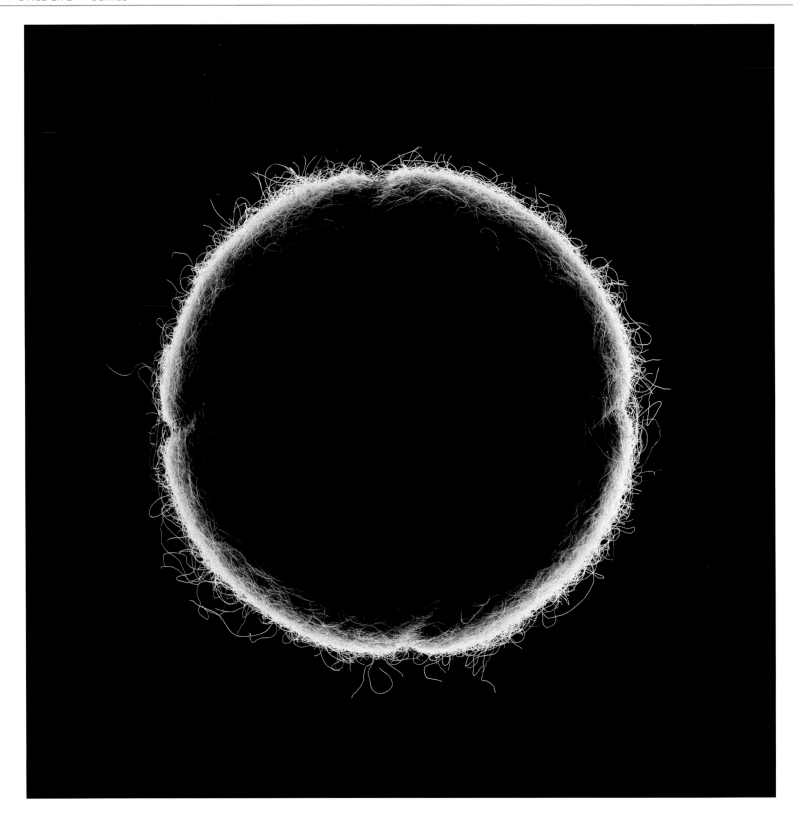

LOL KEEGAN

PRINTER: Lol Keegan

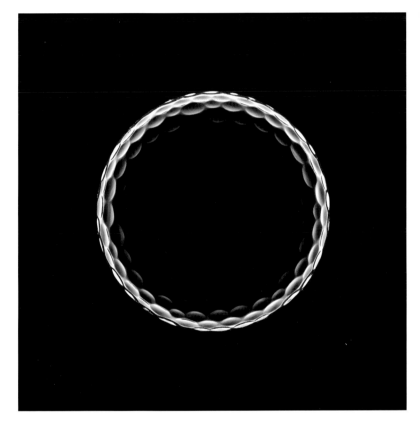

Name	Telephone	Page	Name	Telephone	Page
Alvarez, Pedro	07966 524161	264	Stewart, Andy	020 7635 7609	274
Andrews, Meredith	07932 042495	215	Stuart, Graeme	07818 404454	221
Bartle, Nicholas	07970 997559	272	Walsh, Nicky	07734 217693	268
Bentley, Dave	07977 050201	228	White, Greg	07769 586525	222, 261
Braune, Rik	+31 647 894938	210	Winkley, Mark	07961 454837	252
Brodie, Matthew	07786 163412	246			
Christmas, Sam	07946 700419	238, 244, 248			
Day, Jon	07989 558107	212			
Denny, David	+44 (0)7973 739090	256			
Farrant, Matthew	+44 (0)7801 643966	216			
Ferrari, Armando A D	07801 490700	258			
Goldblatt, Lydia	07779 632350	217			
Hicks, Samuel	07966 255396	211, 218, 230, 259			
Irby, Caroline	+44 7967 659043	226			
Keegan, Lol	07976 731591	277			
Koch, Simone	07754 905324	273			
Mentz, Hannah	07941 092987	219			
Micah Miller, Joel	+44 179 703 4575	242			
Mills, Phil	+44 (0)7973 430968	213			
Mitchell, Emma	07973 421920	250			
Murphy, Spencer	07811 139704	232, 266			
Redman, Joel	07970 617797	220, 239			
Richards, Roger	07973 734013	260			
Rigby, Andy	07985 248637	234			
Schofield, Soraya	07980 923676	257			
Stagg, Jesse	07798 800468	214			

THE AOP WOULD LIKE TO THANK THE FOLLOWING
PEOPLE WHO HAVE GIVEN THEIR TIME, SKILL AND
EXPERTISE, AND THE MEMBERSHIP OF THE AOP
WHOSE SUPPORT MAKES THESE AWARDS POSSIBLE

PHOTOGRAPHY AWARDS 2004 JUDGES

Jonathan Anderson
Sophie Batterbury
Suzanne Bisset
Desmond Burdon
Nigel Clifton
Alan Dye
Tim Flach
David Gardiner
Nadav Kander
Edwin Lowe
Sung Ma
Simon Norfolk
Nigel Rose
Joanne Smith
Tabitha Wilson

PHOTOGRAPHY AWARDS 2004 COMMITTEE

Tim Flach (chair)
Anthony Marsland
Alistair Berg
Adri Berger
Jay Myrdal
Brian Stuart
Paul Wakefield

PHOTOGRAPHY AWARDS 2004 ORGANISERS

Nicola Waterhouse (Awards Manager)
Jonathan Briggs
(Head of Publications & Marketing)
James McCarthy
(Website & Database Officer)
Jackie Kelley
(For help and guidance)

PHOTOGRAPHY AWARDS 2004 PROGRAMME

Holbrooks Printers
Telephone +44 (0)23 9266 1485

PHOTOGRAPHY AWARDS 2004 PHOTOGRAPHER

Photo: Matt Wreford

Eric Richmond:
an American-born
photographer, specialising
in shooting posters for arts
organisations. His clients
include the Royal Opera House,
English National Ballet and
Rambert Dance Company.
Other commissions include
posters for West End theatre
productions, CD covers,
publicity photos for various
orchestras, actors, singers
and musicians.

Tel: +(44) 208 8806909
E-mail: eric@ericrichmond.net
Web: www.ericrichmond.net

CHUBB

EPSON®

gettyimages®

Kodak Professional

[magnet harlequin]

M **e** T **r** O

MOT MODELS

Resolution Creative
www.resolveandcreate.co.uk

www.taylorjames.com

z | e | f | a |